Resources for Teaching Mathematics: 11–14

Also available in the Resources for Teaching Series

Resources for Teaching Mathematics: 14–16, Colin Foster

Resources for Teaching English: 11–14, Helena Ceranic

Resources for Teaching English: 14–16, David A. Hill

Resources for Teaching French: 14–16, James Gill

Resources for Teaching History: 11–14, Susie Hodge

Resources for Teaching History: 14–16, Susie Hodge

Resources for Teaching Shakespeare: 11–16, Fred Sedgwick

Also available from Continuum

50 Mathematics Lessons, Colin Foster

The Mathematics Teacher's Handbook, Mike Ollerton

Teaching Mathematics Using ICT, Adrian Oldknow, Ron Taylor and Linda Tetlow

Resources for Teaching Mathematics: 11–14

Colin Foster

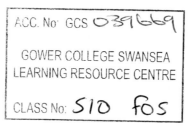

continuum

Continuum International Publishing Group

The Tower Building	80 Maiden Lane
11 York Road	Suite 704
London	New York
SE1 7NX	NY 10038

www.continuumbooks.com

British Library Cataloguing-in-Publication Data
A catalogue record for this book is available from the British Library.

ISBN: 978-1-4411-4227-6 (paperback)

Library of Congress Cataloging-in-Publication Data
Foster, Colin, 1973-
Resources for teaching mathematics, 11–14 / Colin Foster.
        p. cm. — (Resources for teaching)
    "A companion website to accompany this book is available online at: <http://education. foster2.continuumbooks.com/>http://education.foster2.continuumbooks.com."
    ISBN 978-1-4411-4227-6 (pbk.)
    1. Mathematics—Study and teaching (Middle school) 2. Lesson planning. 3. Curriculum planning. I. Title.
    QA135.6.F678 2010
    510.71'2—dc22   2011005127

Contents

Acknowledgements — vii

Introduction — viii

1 Amazing Ways — 1
Counting the numbers of routes through a word maze

2 Dividing Cakes — 6
Partitioning fractions in different ways

3 Draw a Picture — 10
Drawing pictures using mathematical graphs

4 Ever-Increasing Circles — 14
Approximating the area of a circle by counting dots

5 Factor Trees — 18
Exploring patterns in prime factor trees

6 Fiddling Averages — 22
Investigating how averages can be manipulated

7 Folding — 26
Finding connections relating to flat folds

8 Four Numbers — 30
Generating and solving linear equations

9 Four Weights — 34
Making as many values as possible from four numbers

10 Four-Star Hotels — 38
Deducing the contents of a grid from the sums of columns and rows

11 Fuel — 42
Maximizing the amount of fuel that can be transferred across a desert

12 Have a Megaday! — 46
Converting time units and using standard prefixes

13 How Far? — 50
Devising a statistical experiment

14 Infinity — 54
Exploring a converging sequence

15 Investigating Mirrors — 58
Finding out what happens when you reflect more than once

16 Journey Through a Word — 62
Using bearings and distance to describe a route

17 Ladders — 66
Solving simultaneous equations and drawing straight-line graphs

18 Make Twenty-Four — 70
Using priority of operations to construct calculations

19 Meeting Up — 74
Finding out how straight lines relate to their equations

20 Mystery Messages — 78
Using frequency analysis to crack a substitution code

21 Newspaper Pages — 82
Investigating the pagination of newspapers and books

22 One Cut — 86
Categorizing the outcomes from one fold and one cut of a square

23 Palindromic Numbers — 90
Solving problems relating to palindromic numbers

24 Percentage Puzzles — 94
Practising mental percentage calculations

25 Pizza Slices — 98
Finding the areas and perimeters of circular sectors

26 Rectilinear Shapes — 102
Exploring angles and line segments in rectilinear shapes

27 Regular Polygons — 106
Understanding necessary and sufficient conditions in geometry

28 Seven Divided by Three   110
Partitioning integers and finding patterns

29 Shape Riddles   114
Understanding inclusive definitions

30 Shapes within Shapes   118
*Relating numerical sequences to
geometrical properties*

31 Sharing Camels   122
*Using fractions to solve a remainder
problem*

32 Simultaneous Investigation   126
*Finding simultaneous equations with
integer solutions*

33 Sinusoids   130
Examining the sine and cosine graphs

34 Squares and Remainders   134
*Exploring the divisibility properties of
square numbers*

35 Squares and Roots   138
*Finding out how square numbers and surds
behave*

36 Star Polygons   142
*Calculating angles in star polygons and
drawing them*

37 Street Race   146
Using travel graphs to solve problems

38 Symmetrical Possibilities   150
*Finding examples of shapes with specified
symmetries*

39 Take a Breath   154
*Estimating and calculating using large
numbers*

40 The Playground Problem   158
Solving a practical minimization problem

41 The Tailor's Rule of Thumb   162
*Testing statistical hypotheses relating to
body proportions*

42 The Totient Function   166
Investigating patterns in reducible fractions

43 Three Consecutive Numbers   170
Using algebra to prove relationships

44 Transforming Graphs   174
*Carrying out transformations on straight-
line graphs*

45 Transport Problems   178
*Solving complicated problems in the best
possible way*

46 Trapped Squares   182
*Exploring patterns relating to straight-line
graphs*

47 Travel Arrangements   186
Making and interpreting travel graphs

48 Triangle Angles   190
*Using simple trigonometry to solve not-so-
simple triangles*

49 Vanishing Lines   194
*Explaining an optical illusion using
gradient*

50 Water   198
*Calculating volumes and lengths and
finding connections*

Other Resources   202
Index   203

Acknowledgements

I would like to thank Peter Booth for permission to use data from his website http://home.manhattan.edu/~peter.boothe/ in Lesson 18.

I would like to thank the teams at Continuum and Pindar NZ for all their hard work and Megan Gay (Year 11) for drawing several of the pictures. I would particularly like to thank John Cooper and Tim Honeywill, together with many other colleagues, for numerous helpful conversations relating to these ideas. Most of all, I would like to thank the many learners who have given their energies to these tasks and taught me more about how people learn mathematics.

Introduction

Resources for Teaching Mathematics 11–14 comprises 50 lesson plans covering many of the topics commonly encountered at this age. The lessons seek to draw learners into thinking about the various ideas by involving them in tasks that are not straightforward or routine. Learners of any level of prior attainment can gain satisfaction from thinking carefully about worthwhile mathematics and, in the hands of a skilful teacher, these tasks can work well for all learners, however they may be grouped or setted. Much of the material is designed to be divergent, with learners self-differentiating according to their current skills, interest, speed or mood. It is to be expected that different learners, beginning with the same starting point, will finish in quite different places. 'Answers' are given for the teacher's convenience rather than to suggest that they should be the optimum endpoint for everyone. It helps if the teacher is not too rigid in his/her mind about what the 'proper' route should be or how far learners must get during a particular lesson. The notion of 'finishing off' is problematic for many mathematics teachers when working with rich tasks, since when a mathematician answers one question they are likely to find themselves asking others.

The lessons are described under headings that indicate a possible beginning of the lesson ('starter'), a middle (some kind of 'main lesson') and a suggested whole-class discussion to end ('plenary'), but clearly a successful mathematics lesson does not have to follow that pattern slavishly. Beginning with a plenary or having one or more mini-plenaries in the middle, or omitting a starter, etc., are all viable options, so there is no need to be too regimented about such matters. The teacher should not feel dictated to by resources such as this book and must be free to adapt material, responding to learners' progress, comments, questions and interests, and using their skills to lead the lesson in the most beneficial way possible. A photocopiable Task Sheet is provided for each lesson to help learners engage with the tasks at their own pace. Likely outcomes and objectives are indicated to help the teacher to think in advance about what may arise and what opportunities are available. Possible homework tasks are suggested, as are ways of extending the tasks for early-finishers or those very confident with the ideas. There are also suggestions of ways in which a learner who finds the work particularly difficult might begin.

On many occasions in these lessons, learners are asked to generate their own mathematical examples. This can be beneficial by encouraging them to see what possibilities are available within the particular mathematical structure. Additionally, they also give the teacher valuable information, enabling him/her to assess the depth and breadth of a learner's understanding at that moment. What learners choose to create tells you about what possibilities they are aware of and able to access. Techniques such as specializing and generalizing in a problem-solving context are central to working on mathematics and are encouraged on many occasions.

Human beings possess the capacity to solve demanding problems and work with complex situations. The mathematical tasks presented in this book seek to draw on learners' innate abilities to make sense out of situations – to bring order out of chaos. Some of the material will be highly challenging, but if learners can be encouraged to struggle without giving up, and are given the time and freedom necessary to dig into the ideas, they can get a lot out of working with rich problems. Sometimes teachers feel under pressure to over-simplify and to try to turn every area of mathematics into a stepwise list of rules, so that 'methods' come from the teacher and the learners' responsibility is merely to memorize and reproduce them on demand. If this happens, lessons are likely to degenerate into 'demonstration by the teacher' followed by 'practice' by the learners. Such a structure does not harness the natural mathematical talents that young people possess and tends to be unrewarding for everyone involved.

Some of the questions and prompts on the resource sheets are linguistically demanding and learners who find this a barrier are likely to need in-class support in order to access the materials fully. At times the wording may appear vague, but this is in an attempt to move away from rigid instructions and provide space for learners to interpret things in their own way and structure their own work. These lessons will succeed if learners and teachers are not trying to finish them as quickly as possible but instead are attempting to look around for interesting avenues and generate questions and ideas of their own as they go.

The questions and prompts intended directly for learners are displayed in *italics* throughout the teacher notes. All of the Task Sheets are available online and other online resources are indicated by the mouse symbol.

Colin Foster

March 2011

Amazing Ways

Introduction

'Maze' word puzzles, similar to the ones used in this lesson, appear frequently in puzzle books and newspapers. One way to tackle them is simply to try to count all the possibilities. However, being more systematic can save a lot of time, improve accuracy and enable an appreciation of the structure. The one presented on the Task Sheet is intended to be large enough to discourage simple counting and provoke a more thoughtful approach.

Aims and outcomes

- Count systematically and reason logically.
- Investigate a structure related to Pascal's triangle.

Lesson starter (15 minutes)

What do you see when you look at this?

```
                  S
               S  H  S
            S  H  T  H  S
         S  H  T  A  T  H  S
      S  H  T  A  M  A  T  H  S
```

It may take some time before learners see more than one occurrence of the word 'MATHS'. Learners could come to the board to show a spelling of 'MATHS' with their finger.

How many ways are there of 'doing MATHS' here?

Different learners could show different routes. There are 31 ways, but this answer is likely to come later.

Can you be sure that you have found them all?

One way would be to simplify the problem – it would be easier in countries which call the subject 'MATH', so we could start by losing the 'S'. Learners could begin by finding ways of doing 'MA', then 'MAT', then 'MATH'.

Main lesson (25 minutes)

Give out the Task Sheets. 'MATHEMATICS' is much too long a word to do by counting. You could focus learners' attention on the number of ways of arriving at any particular *letter* on the grid (shown with numbers over the page), or leave learners to find this for themselves.

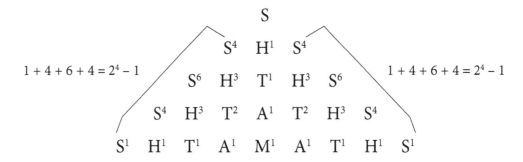

$$1 + 4 + 6 + 4 = 2^4 - 1$$

$$1 + 4 + 6 + 4 = 2^4 - 1$$

To arrive at any of the letters in the right-hand side of the grid, all movements must be either upwards (U) or right (R), so instructions such as UUR would represent a $\binom{2}{1}$ shift from the starting M to an H. Since there are $^3C_1$ ways of permuting two Us and an R, there are this many (3) ways of arriving at this H. So the positions in the grid are the binomial coefficients ^nC_r from Pascal's triangle. (The left-hand side works similarly using upwards and *left*.) Learners may see that to arrive at a particular letter necessitates having come from one position to the side or one position down, and therefore the number of ways of getting there must be the sum of the number of ways of getting to these two positions. Alternatively, looking at the right-hand side of the diagram, there are two ways of getting to either of the As, and then, whichever A you are on, there are two ways of getting to a T, and so on, giving 2^4 ways of getting to any of the six Ss on the right. Since there will also be 2^4 ways of getting to the six Ss on the left, we just need to subtract 1 for the top S (which we have counted twice) to get $2(2^4) - 1 = 2^5 - 1 = 31$ ways.

Plenary (15 minutes)

Which words did you try? Why? How many ways did you find? What did you notice?

Learners may observe symmetries that make it easier to calculate the total number of ways – such as dividing the diagram into halves or quarters. Learners may comment on the fact that the letters M, A, T and H all have a vertical line of symmetry, and so a diagram based on MA, MAT or MATH will have a vertical line of symmetry through the M. Learners may notice that the total number of ways must be an odd number, since all routes have a partner found by reflecting in the vertical line through the M; however, there is also the straight-up path from M, which adds an additional 1, making the total number of ways odd.

For MATHS, taking this approach gives that the total number of ways = $2(2^4 - 1) + 1 = 2^5 - 1 = 31$, as before. In general, for an *n*-letter word, number of ways = $2^n - 1$.

n	Number of ways
1	1
2	3
3	7
4	15
5	31
6	63
7	127
8	255
9	511
10	1023
11	2047

So, the answer for MATHEMATICS (with 11 letters) is 2047. Learners may notice that each answer is the previous answer multiplied by 2 and add 1.

If we allow the letters to continue *downwards* as well, we obtain:

```
                  S
              S   H   S
          S   H   T   H   S
      S   H   T   A   T   H   S
  S   H   T   A   M   A   T   H   S
      S   H   T   A   T   H   S
          S   H   T   H   S
              S   H   S
                  S
```

Here, number of ways = $4(2^4 - 1) = 2^6 - 4 = 60$. In general, for an *n*-letter word, the number of ways = $4(2^{n-1} - 1)$.

n	Number of ways
1	1
2	4
3	12
4	28
5	60
6	124
7	252
8	508
9	1020
10	2044
11	4092

So the answer for MATHEMATICS this time is 4092. In this situation, from the second value onwards, each term is the previous one multiplied by 2 and add 4.

Do all five-letter words, say, have the same number of ways?

Double letters may lead to some discussion, since *diagonal* moves now (perhaps) become possible, if this is allowed, leading to many more routes (two shown below, for the word MEET):

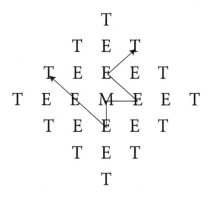

Including diagonal moves, there are now $8 \times 3.5 \times 2.5 = 70$ ways.

Palindromic words (words which read the same forwards and backwards) are also interesting. Learners may think that they will simply have twice as many ways, since each route can be traced in either direction, but there are more than this, since the word now does not have to begin or end at the centre of the diagram. A three-letter palindrome, such as TOT, has 48 ways, but a four-letter palindrome such as TOOT (which necessarily has a double letter in the middle) has, ignoring diagonal moves, exactly twice as many ways as MATH (i.e. 56 ways). A five-letter palindrome, such as LEVEL, however, has 228 ways, if you count cyclic routes in which the first and final L are the same position.

Homework (5 minutes)

Learners could attempt to make up and solve similar problems on *isometric* grids.

To make it harder

Confident learners could extend the idea into three dimensions, creating an octahedron of letters.

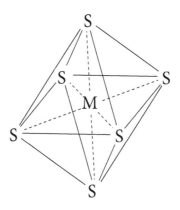

The contribution of the 'equatorial' Ss will be $2^6 - 4$, as for the 2D case. There are eight more edges, each contributing $2^4 - 2$ ('subtract 2' since we have already counted the 'equatorial' S of each one). Then there are two further Ss at the apexes. So the total number of ways of reading MATHS will be $2^6 - 4 + 8(2^4 - 2) + 2 = 174$. The same approach with an *n*-letter word, shows that, in general, the total number of ways $= 6(2^n - 3)$.

n	Number of ways
1	1
2	6
3	30
4	78
5	174
6	366
7	750
8	1518
9	3054
10	6126
11	12 270

To make it easier

Starting with a short word, such as MAT, should be accessible to all learners.

Amazing Ways

```
                        S
                      S C S
                    S C I C S
                  S C I T I C S
                S C I T A T I C S
              S C I T A M A T I C S
            S C I T A M E M A T I C S
          S C I T A M E H E M A T I C S
        S C I T A M E H T H E M A T I C S
      S C I T A M E H T A T H E M A T I C S
    S C I T A M E H T A M A T H E M A T I C S
  S C I T A M E H T A M A T H E M A T I C S
    S C I T A M E H T A T H E M A T I C S
      S C I T A M E H T H E M A T I C S
        S C I T A M E H E M A T I C S
          S C I T A M E M A T I C S
            S C I T A M A T I C S
              S C I T A T I C S
                S C I T I C S
                  S C I C S
                    S C S
                      S
```

What do you see when you look at this diagram?

How many ways do you think there are of finding MATHEMATICS in this diagram? Why?

How can you be sure that you have found them all?

What do you think would happen if you used a shorter or longer word? Why?

What happens with *double* letters?

What if you used a *palindrome* (a word that reads the same forwards and backwards), like ROTAVATOR?

Dividing Cakes

Introduction

Does $\frac{1}{2} + \frac{1}{2} = 1$? Mathematically, of course, yes, but in real life two broken half computers do not make one whole working machine; two half-accurate statements do not add up to one accurate statement. Similarly, with many classic 'real-life mathematics' sharing problems, although the fractional pieces may, in theory, add up to the same amount, they are not necessarily equally acceptable to those involved. You expect to pay less for a bag of broken biscuits than you do for the same mass of undamaged product! This lesson uses this idea as an opportunity for finding different decompositions of a certain fractional quantity.

Aims and outcomes

* Add fractions to obtain desired fractional amounts.
* Understand how to partition fractions into different amounts.

Lesson starter (10 minutes)

You have 10 cakes to share equally among 9 people. How would you do it? How many cuts would you have to make? Why?

Learners are likely to suggest something like this: First give everyone one whole cake. Then cut the leftover cake into 9 equal pieces (this is not too hard; you can do thirds and then thirds of thirds). So give each person $\frac{1}{9}$, then everyone has a whole cake and $\frac{1}{9}$ of a cake (i.e. two pieces).

Let's do it the other way round. This time you have 10 people and 9 cakes. What would you do this time?

Learners could think about this in groups. You could cut $\frac{1}{10}$ out of each of the nine cakes. Then 9 of the people each get the remaining $\frac{9}{10}$ of these nine cakes. The ninth person gets all 9 of the separate $\frac{1}{10}$ pieces.

Is this fair?

'Fairness' means different things to different people. Maybe some people are bigger, older or more important (or all three!) or are allergic to or don't like cake, etc. So it would be good to ask learners what they think counts as fair. Here everyone gets the same amount of cake, but nine of the people get almost a complete cake, and one person just gets a heap of crumbs! Learners might suggest cutting each cake into eighths, say, so that 9 people get $\frac{7}{8}$ each and the person with the bits gets $\frac{9}{8} = 1\frac{1}{8}$, which is a little more, so as to compensate for the 'crumbiness' of their portion.

Main lesson (30 minutes)

Come up with a better solution, so that everyone gets exactly *the same – not just the same amount of cake but the same number and size of pieces: indistinguishable portions. Try to make as little mess as possible (as few cuts as you can).*

 Give out the Task Sheets and encourage learners to think hard about this problem. Learners may suggest cutting *all* nine cakes into tenths and giving each person nine separate tenths. This satisfies the fairness aspect but is obviously messy, wasteful and time-consuming. So you might want to encourage learners also to minimise the number of cuts.

Plenary (15 minutes)

What did you work out? What were your ideas?

Learners may suggest things like baking another cake or drawing lots to decide as fairly as possible who should get the inferior portion. But we are aiming to make nine equal-in-every-respect portions.

One solution is to give each person $\frac{1}{2} + \frac{2}{5}$. Other possible solutions, for 10 cakes but different numbers of people, are shown in the table below

Number of cakes number of people	Possible fractions given to each person
$\frac{9}{10}$	$\frac{1}{2} + \frac{1}{5}$
	$\frac{1}{2} + \frac{1}{3} + \frac{1}{15}$
$\frac{8}{10} \left(= \frac{4}{5} \right)$	$\frac{1}{2} + \frac{1}{4} + \frac{1}{20}$
	$\frac{1}{2} + \frac{1}{5} + \frac{1}{10}$
$\frac{7}{10}$	$\frac{1}{2} + \frac{1}{5}$
$\frac{6}{10} \left(= \frac{3}{5} \right)$	$\frac{1}{2} + \frac{1}{10}$
$\frac{5}{10} \left(= \frac{1}{2} \right)$	$\frac{1}{2}$

Learners may comment on the 'sacrifice' that some people are making, in terms of the quality of their cake portions, for the sake of equality for everyone, and this could relate to learners' views on society and egalitarianism.

Homework (5 minutes)

Find out about *Egyptian fractions* and what they have to do with this problem. Learners could be asked to make a poster about it. A good website is: www.maths.surrey.ac.uk/hosted-sites/R.Knott/Fractions/egyptian.html

To make it harder

There should be plenty of depth in this problem for all learners. A related problem to consider is to work out the maximum number of pieces you can cut a circular cake into with n straight-line cuts. The answer is the so-called *lazy caterer's sequence*: 2, 4, 7, 11, 16, . . . which fit the formula $^nC_2 + {}^nC_1 + {}^nC_0 = \frac{1}{2}(n^2 + n + 2)$. In *three* dimensions, you have a *cylindrical* cake divided into n plane slices, and this gives $^nC_3 + {}^nC_2 + {}^nC_1 + {}^nC_0 = \frac{1}{6}(n^3 + 5n + 6)$ pieces as the maximum number you can make; the so-called *cake numbers*.

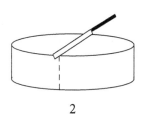

2

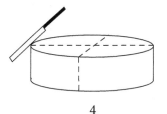

4

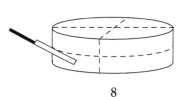

8

To make it easier

Learners who find this hard could start with dividing 3 cakes among 4 people, in which case each person can have one half and one quarter. Then move to 3 cakes among 5 people ($\frac{1}{2} + \frac{1}{10}$ each).

Dividing Cakes

Share 9 cakes among 10 people so that everybody gets *exactly the same portion*, not just the same amount of cake.

Try to use as few cuts as possible.

What happens with a different number of cakes?

What happens with a different number of people?

3

Draw a Picture

Introduction

This lesson relies on each learner (or pair of learners) having access to a computer running graph-drawing software, such as *Omnigraph* or *Autograph*, or a graphical calculator. Learners will work on making pictures using mathematical equations, particularly circle equations. Often learners will get close to what they want and then have to tweak it – moving a curve up a little or to the left or enlarging it. On other occasions, the curve will not appear at all as the learner wished and they will have to work out what has happened. This is where their sense of how the equations relate to the drawings will develop.

Aims and outcomes

- Know how the equation of a curve relates to its appearance.
- Know how varying a, b and r in the equation $(x - a)^2 + (y - b)^2 = r^2$ of a circle affects the circle.

Lesson starter (10 minutes)

If you have access to graph-drawing software and a data projector, enter $y = x^2 + y^3$ and ask learners to describe what they see.

It is likely that someone will suggest that it looks like a person; if not, you could do so.

What do we need to add?

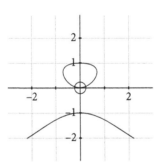

Take learners' suggestions and, by adding suitable curves (e.g. circles, ellipses or whatever learners are familiar with), you can end up with something like this:

(For more information, see Foster, C. (2007) 'Introducing . . . Maths-man!', *Mathematics in School*, 36, (1), 15.)

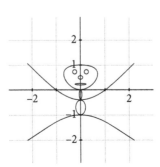

Main lesson (35 minutes)

Give out the Task Sheets. Learners can use any equations that they know about, or experiment to see what is possible. However, circles are likely to be very useful, particularly if learners realize (or are told) that adding constants p and q into the standard equation $(x - a)^2 + (y - b)^2 = r^2$, creating $p(x - a)^2 + q(y - b)^2 = r^2$, generates *ellipses*. (Strictly speaking, only one of p and q is needed, since the other is equivalent to varying r; however, it may be more convenient to have both.)

You may need to assist learners in finding their curves if they are off the screen, using the zoom in/out features.

Plenary (10 minutes)

Rather than having a whole-class discussion, it might be better to invite learners to print out or save their completed drawings and use these for display purposes. If it is possible to print them out during the lesson, they could be placed around the room and learners could have a 'walking plenary', looking at and commenting on each other's work.

How did you do that? How did you change the equation to make that happen?

Homework (5 minutes)

Write about the types of equations you used and how you varied them. Summarize what happens when you change the constants in the equation of a circle.

Learners could also find out more about ellipses and their equations.

To make it harder

There are no limits to the opportunities here for more complicated equations and curves.

To make it easier

Learners who find this task difficult can be encouraged to experiment with the computer, entering different equations and seeing what happens. Reassure them that they can always 'undo' anything that they don't like or that doesn't work. Drawing different-sized circles in different positions on a blank set of axes could be a useful way to begin.

Draw a Picture

Choose one of the shapes below and put the equation into a graph-drawing program.
Add other equations to 'improve' the pictures by adding detail.

Butterfly: $x^6 + y^6 = x^2$

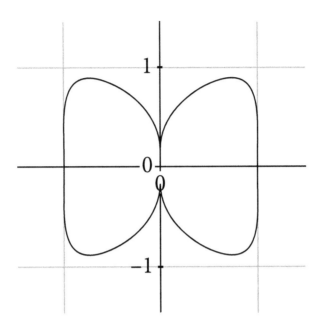

Aeroplane: $(1-y)^2 + (x+4)^{\frac{1}{2}} = \dfrac{3}{3-y}$

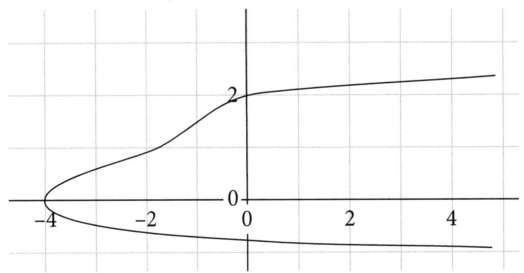

© Colin Foster (2011)   *Resources for Teaching Mathematics 11–14*. London: Continuum

Head: $y^2 = (1 - x^2)^2 (4x^2 - 1)^2 \cos^2 x$

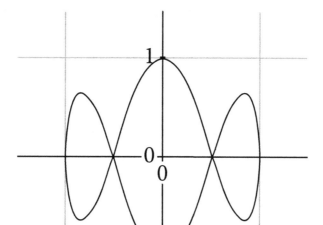

Quadrifolium: $(x^2 + y^2)^3 = 4x^2y^2$

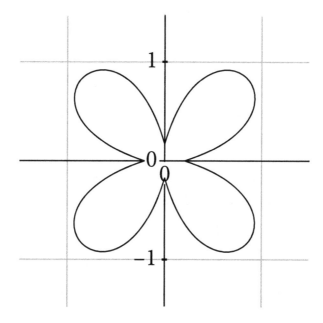

See what happens if you make changes to these equations.

What other drawings can you make using mathematical graphs?

Are there any shapes that you cannot make?

4

Ever-Increasing Circles

Introduction

The *Gauss circle problem* provides an interesting investigation, touching different areas of the curriculum but leading to an appreciation of the area formula for a circle. This could be useful even with learners who already are familiar with the formula. There are opportunities to think about the convergence of sequences in a geometrical context and to use Pythagoras' theorem to justify why a particular point must lie exactly on a particular circle.

Aims and outcomes

- Calculate the area of a circle.
- Investigate sequences for possible convergence.
- Use Pythagoras' theorem to decide whether a circle passes *exactly* through a point.

Lesson starter (10 minutes)

Close your eyes. Imagine a circle with fixed radius r. Divide it into eight equal sectors. Separate all eight pieces. Line them all up, pointing straight upwards, with their curvy portions side by side. Can you imagine it? Describe what you have? What do you see at the bottom? What do you see at the top?

Learners should be able to talk about the eight one-eighth arcs along the bottom and the eight spikes all lined up along the top.

Open your eyes. Suppose that we slice the circle into more *sectors, arrange the pieces the same way as before and then shear horizontally:*

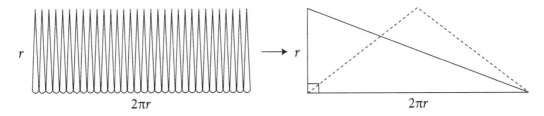

You can get (almost) an isosceles (dotted) or a right-angled (solid) triangle, as shown above.

How long is the base of the triangle?

It is the circumference of the circle, $2\pi r$.

How high is it?

It is the radius, r.

So the area of the triangle (either of them) is $\frac{(2\pi r)r}{2} = \pi r^2$. The more sectors the original circle is sliced into, the more closely the pieces will fit to make these triangles. So we can make this process as accurate as we like by taking more and more pieces. With 'infinitely many' pieces, it will be exact.

Main lesson (30 minutes)

Give out the Task Sheets. Encourage learners to count carefully and try to be sure about whether dots lie *exactly on* the circle or not.

Plenary (15 minutes)

What results did you get? Were there any dots that you were unsure about? Which ones? Why?

Each circle has at least four points lying on it, where it crosses the axes. The circle with radius $r = 5$ has an additional eight points (i.e. 12 altogether), such as $(3, 4)$ and $(4, 3)$, in the first quadrant, since $3^2 + 4^2 = 5^2$. Similarly, the circle with radius $r = 10$ has an additional eight points (i.e. 12 altogether, again), such as $(6, 8)$ and $(8, 6)$, since $6^2 + 8^2 = 10^2$. Other points, such as $(9, 1)$ and $(7, 4)$, that *look* as though they might lie on a circle do not in fact. (Learners can check that $9^2 + 1^2 \neq 9^2$ and $7^2 + 4^2 \neq 8^2$, although they are close!)

There are some interesting patterns in the number of dots:

Radius, r	Number of dots inside	Number of dots on the circle	Total number of dots	Total/r^2 (correct to 3 significant figures)
0	0	1	1	error
1	1	4	5	5.00
2	9	4	13	3.25
3	25	4	29	3.22
4	45	4	49	3.06
5	69	12	81	3.24
6	109	4	113	3.14
7	145	4	149	3.04
8	193	4	197	3.08
9	249	4	253	3.12
10	305	12	317	3.17

Learners may notice that it hits 3.14 (correct to 3 significant figures) and then drifts away before coming back – such is the nature of converging sequences. It seems to be converging to a value that could be π.

Homework (5 minutes)

Learners could find out about the life of Georg Pick (1859–1942) and about his theorem (Pick's theorem). They could also look into circle-packing and circle-covering problems, perhaps collecting some facts to share next lesson.

To make it harder

Confident learners might like to decide whether it is better to *include* the dots that are exactly on the circle or to count only the *interior* ones.

They could also consider what the two diagrams below suggest about the area of a circle:

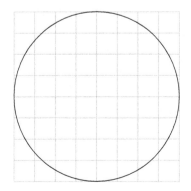 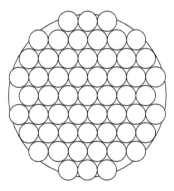

For the first diagram, learners could count squares (and perhaps part-squares) to obtain an approximation for π. For the second diagram, the large circle has radius 4 cm and contains 55 circles, each of diameter 1 cm, giving an approximation to π of $\frac{55}{4^2} = 3.4375$.

To make it easier

All learners should be able to begin by counting the number of dots in the first few circles. It might avoid confusion if they cross out with a pencil the ones they have counted.

Ever-Increasing Circles

Look at these concentric circles.

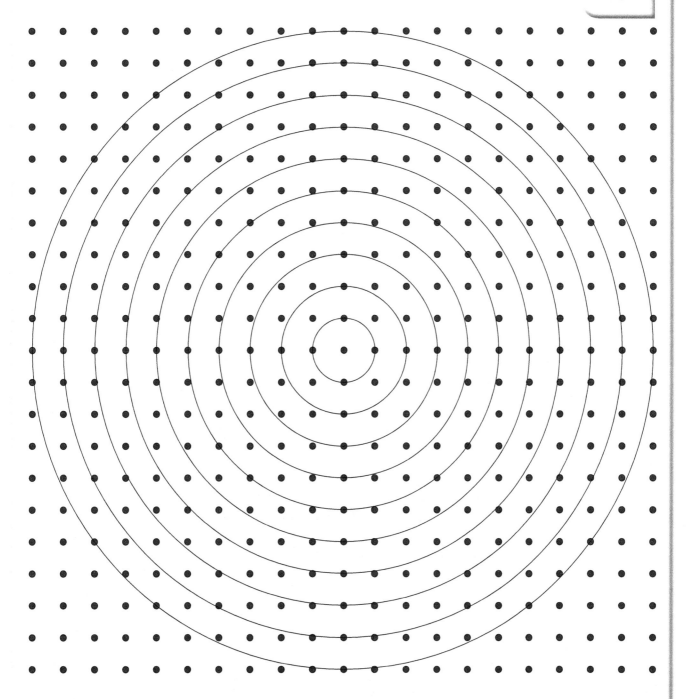

How many of the dots lie *exactly* on a circle?

How can you be sure?

Write down the number of dots on each circle.

Make a table showing the number of dots *on* and *inside* each circle.

What do your results show you?

5

Factor Trees

Introduction

Prime factorization reveals what it is that makes prime numbers so special: they are the building blocks of all of our integers. Every non-prime integer can be broken down into a product of prime numbers – and in only one way (other than by changing the order of the factors). This makes it clear why we do not consider 1 to be a prime number. Although you might say that it has factors of 'one and itself' (since 'itself' is 1), it is not a useful building block in multiplication, since multiplying by 1 does not change the value of a number. In this lesson, learners get lots of practice at prime factorizing and consider removing factors in different orders – always arriving at the same factorization in the end.

Aims and outcomes

- Consider the unique factorization of the integers into primes.
- Prime factorize a given number.

Lesson starter (10 minutes)

Write the number '1000' on the board. *Can you find two integers that multiply together to make 1000, neither of which contains any zeroes?*

Learners may think that it is impossible at first, but there is one possible solution: 8×125. If anyone gets this quickly, ask them to try 10 000 or 100 000 or 1 000 000. *What patterns do you find?*

A variation of this problem is to ask for two numbers that multiply to make 10^n, neither of which *ends* in a zero. This is *always* possible, for any positive integer n, since, in general, $10^n = 2^n \times 5^n$, and neither 2^n nor 5^n can ever end in a zero (since 10 cannot be a factor of either). However, many powers of 2 and of 5 will *contain* a zero. The first power of 2 which *contains* a zero is $2^{10} = 1024$, and the first power of 5 that *contains* a zero is $5^8 = 390\,625$, so it is possible to have *no* zeroes in either number for all powers of 10 up to and including 10^7, but it will also work for some higher powers, such as 10^{18}, for instance, which is $262\,144 \times 3\,814\,697\,265\,625$.

Main lesson (30 minutes)

Write '1000' in the middle of the board, with 8 and 125 underneath.

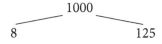

What if we carry on this process with 8 and 125?

The diagram may continue as below:

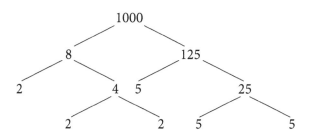

What happens now?

You cannot proceed any further with integers: writing $2 = 1 \times 2$ would go on forever and not lead to any new numbers, so we don't regard 1 as prime and we stop here, with prime numbers. So $1000 = 2^3 \times 5^3$.

At what points do we have choices *along the way?*

We could use '1' as one of the factors each time, but that doesn't reduce the number at all – we get caught in an infinite loop of splitting n into 1 and n repeatedly. We have a choice about *order* when we write '2, 4' under '8' instead of '4, 2', but with $25 = 5 \times 5$ we have no choice of order.

There are 10 branches (line segments) on this tree and 4 'levels': '1000' in the top level, then '8, 125' in the second level, then '2, 4, 5, 25' in the third level and finally '2, 2, 5, 5' in the fourth level.

Give out the Task Sheets and encourage learners to try to cover all possibilities.

Plenary (15 minutes)

Since $1000 = 2 \times 500 = 4 \times 250 = 5 \times 200 = 8 \times 125 = 10 \times 100 = 20 \times 50 = 25 \times 40$, there will be 7 possibilities for the second level of the tree. In general, if we start with n, which can be expressed as $n = p^a q^b r^c \ldots$, where $p, q, r, \ldots$ are prime factors and a, b, c are positive integer indices, then since in the factors of n we can have $p^0, p^1, p^2, \ldots$ all the way up to p^a (and similarly for $q, r, \ldots$), there will be $(a + 1)(b + 1)(c + 1) \ldots$ factors of n in total. For example, for $1000 = 2^3 \times 5^3$, there will be $(3 + 1)(3 + 1) = 16$ factors, occurring in 8 pairs. Since we are excluding 1×1000, there will be 7 possible factor pairs of 1000 in the second level of the tree, as listed above. In general, there will be $\dfrac{(a + 1)(b + 1)(c + 1) \ldots}{2} - 1$ possible factor pairs for the second level of the tree. If n is a *square* number, then $(a + 1)(b + 1)(c + 1) \ldots$ will be *odd* (since $a, b, c, \ldots$ will all be *even*), so we will need to add 1 before dividing by 2. Alternatively, we can write (for any n) that the number of possible factor pairs $= \left\lceil \dfrac{(a + 1)(b + 1)(c + 1) \ldots}{2} \right\rceil - 1$, where the brackets represent the 'ceiling function' (rounding up to the nearest integer, if necessary). 'Normal rounding up' (before or after the subtracting 1) would be equivalent to this.

Another possibility for 1000 would be the following:

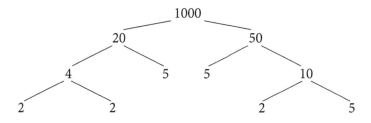

Sometimes learners think that the 'shortest' tree (i.e. the one with fewest levels) comes from splitting each number into factors of as similar size as possible. But this doesn't work when a large prime factor appears to a low power together with a much smaller prime factor to a higher power. For example, $992 = 31 \times 2^5$, but if you split it into 31 and 32 in the second level you end up with the following very lopsided tree and a resulting minimum of 5 levels.

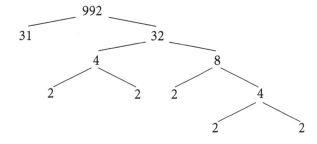

Resources for Teaching Mathematics 11–14

TEACHER SHEET

Splitting differently leads to more symmetry and just 4 levels, the fewest possible for 992:

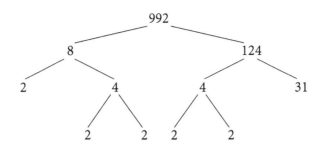

The total number of branches (line segments) depends only on the starting number and not on the details of the particular tree drawn. It is given by $2(a + b + c + \ldots - 1)$, since writing out all of the prime factors, without using index notation, would lead to $(a + b + c + \ldots)$ factors, separated by $(a + b + c + \ldots - 1)$ multiplication signs. Since each multiplication corresponds to two branches, we must therefore have $2(a + b + c + \ldots - 1)$ branches.

The *maximum possible* number of levels will be $(a + b + c + \ldots)$, since in the worst case each level after the second will reveal only one new prime factor. The splitting which leads to the fewest levels is the one which assigns, at each stage, as near to *equal numbers* of prime factors to each 'half' as possible. So with 992 it is best to split into, for example, $124 = 2^2 \times 31$ and $8 = 2^3$, with 3 prime factors each. The minimum possible number of levels is therefore $\left\lceil \dfrac{a + b + c + \ldots}{2} + 1 \right\rceil$. So for $48 = 2^4 \times 3$, the sum of the indices of the prime factors is $4 + 1 = 5$, so the minimum possible number of levels is $\left\lceil \dfrac{5}{2} + 1 \right\rceil = 4$.

Homework (5 minutes)

One challenge is to draw the tree, without any numbers, and ask learners to find a suitable starting number (and factorization order) that will conform to that tree. *Are some tree structures impossible? Why/why not?*

It is possible to do this by starting at the bottom, with the prime numbers, and working upwards. Provided that only two branches come out of each number, any structure will satisfy infinitely many possible numbers.

To make it harder

Confident learners could explore what happens if at each stage a number can be split into either two or three factors; e.g. for 1000 you could have the following, in just three levels.

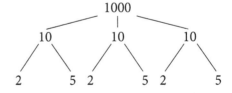

To make it easier

Learners who find this hard could begin with small numbers, such as 6 or 12, exploring the possible trees carefully.

Factor Trees

Here is a factor tree for 1000:

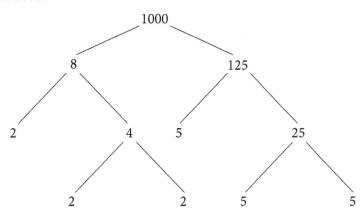

$$1000 = 2^3 \times 5^3$$

What other factor trees can you make for 1000?

How many different factor trees for 1000 do you think are possible? Why?

What is the same and what is different about them?

This factor tree has 10 branches (lines) and takes up four levels.

How many branches and levels do your other factor trees for 1000 have? Why?

What happens with other numbers? What different structures of tree can you get?

Are any structures impossible? Why/why not?

6

Fiddling Averages

Introduction

Statements regarding averages are often misinterpreted, and sometimes there are deliberate attempts at deception. In this lesson, learners are put in the position of trying to deceive someone else with averages. This is not intended to legitimize such behaviour, and the context is intended to be sufficiently absurd as to indicate that it is not to be taken seriously. Instead, it may help learners to be more discerning and sensibly sceptical when interpreting averages. There is an old joke about someone moving from one country to another, thereby raising the average intelligence of both countries. This implies that the person is less intelligent than the average person in the first country but more intelligent than the average person in the second country, and therefore is a dig both at them and at the country they are moving to. This idea forms the basis for the proposed manipulation in this lesson.

Aims and outcomes

- Calculate mean values from given data.
- Consider how group size can affect the significance of average values.
- Explore how average values can be manipulated.

Lesson starter (15 minutes)

Suppose I run a small business and employ five people: my brother and four other people. I pay my brother £100 000 per year, and I pay the four other people £10 000 per year. What is the average wage at my business?

This depends how learners interpret the meaning of the word 'average'. If learners say, 'Which average?', that is a good question, but you could say 'You decide' or 'Can you work them *all* out?' – if that doesn't discourage them from asking questions in the future!

In ordinary life, the word 'average' most commonly means 'mean', but median and mode are other common measures of central tendency, or 'averages'.

$$\text{mean} = \frac{1 \times 100\,000 + 4 \times 10\,000}{5} = £28\,000$$

$$\text{mode} = £10\,000$$

$$\text{median} = \text{3rd value} = £10\,000$$

Why do the values come out differently?

If I need another member of staff, would it be fair if I published this advertisement?

VACANCY
Average salary: £28 000

Do you think it would be fair if a union representative claimed that the average salary at the business was only £10 000?

Unless I have another brother who might come and work for me, it is likely that whoever gets this job will be paid no more than £10 000. You may see indications of learners' political views (or their parents'!) in the ways in which they talk about this. It may also make them wary when interpreting 'average' statements in the future.

Main lesson (25 minutes)

Give out the Task Sheets. The first part should be fairly straightforward – calculating means from given data. You could either check the values as you circulate around the room or have a mini-plenary to discuss what people have got. If learners are not confident about this part, they are likely to be stuck later. The main part of the task is to consider what happens when children are moved from one group to another.

Plenary (15 minutes)

What did you find out? Did anything surprise you?

The mean marks are:

Class				
A	B	C	D	E
79	65	59	51	43

The 'mean of the means' is 59.4.

What 'win-win' moves did you find, which made every *class better off?*

There are many possibilities, such as the following.

	A	B	C	D	E
	65				35
	70	65		60	40
	80	65		60	45
	85	65		60	45
	95	70	65	60	50
					45
					45
					50
					55
					55
					55
Mean (correct to 2 decimal places)	79	66.25	65	60	47.27

Now the 'mean of the means' is 63.50 (correct to 2 decimal places). All such improvements involve having classes of different sizes.

A drastic solution would be to put the top four students alone in each of four of the classes and then all the rest in a 'sink' set (set E):

	A	B	C	D	E
	95	85	80	70	65
					60
					65
					65
					65
					70

(continued)

(continued from previous page)

					55
					55
					60
					60
					65
					45
					45
					50
					55
					60
					35
					40
					45
					45
					50
Mean	95	85	80	70	**55**

The 'mean of the means' is now 77, which is a huge improvement on the situation at the start.

Can you think of any situations in real life where averages could be manipulated to deceive people? Do you think it happens often?

Learners may have specific examples from outside school. It might be interesting to find out how learners feel about the data that the school collects and publishes regarding learner attainment and how these affect (or don't) any setting arrangements you have.

Homework (5 minutes)

Look for examples in everyday life of the use (or misuse) of averages. Keen learners might like to read Huff, D. (1993) *How to Lie with Statistics*. New York: W. W. Norton & Co. An excellent website with up-to-date examples is: www.badscience.net/

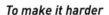

To make it harder

Confident learners could consider the following question.

What if the head teacher says that each class has to have exactly 5 pupils in it. Can he do any fiddling then?

He could prevent any class being lower than 50%, say, but he can't improve the overall average, because any increase in one class will be offset by an equal decrease elsewhere.

Learners who make good progress with this could also consider which kind of average they think is preferable in different situations. For example, when reporting learners' marks in examinations, would it be better to compare them with the 'year mean' or the 'year median', or does it not matter?

There is room for differences of opinion on this, although one answer would be that the median is less affected by outliers and is more straightforward for a parent to interpret, since they can see that half of the learners got a higher mark and half got a lower mark.

To make it easier

Learners who find this confusing may find it helpful to *name* (i.e. label) some of the pupils and then list who is in which class when 'Sharifah', say, has moved from class A to class B. It may help to ask them questions like: 'How many pupils are there in class B now?' if they are inclined to divide by 5 all the time, even when there are not five pupils in the class.

The Dishonest Teacher

© Megan Gay

A teacher is looking at the exam results from five small classes, each containing just five pupils.

Pupil	Class				
	A	B	C	D	E
1	95	70	65	60	50
2	85	65	60	55	45
3	80	65	60	50	45
4	70	65	55	45	40
5	65	60	55	45	35
Mean					

Work out the mean mark for each class and write it in the bottom row of the table.

He thinks that some of the averages look a bit low. Then he has an idea.

'If I take pupil 5 out of class A and put him in class B, I wonder what would happen to the mean scores?'

What will happen to the mean score in class A?
What will happen to the mean score in class C?

Which other pupils could be moved *without reducing any of the means*?
What do you think is the 'best' set of averages he can obtain by shifting pupils around? Why?

7

Folding

Introduction

Folding things up, such as maps, or paper to go in envelopes, is a part of everyday life, even in an age of satellite navigation and email communication. There are some simple and interesting patterns connected with *flat folds*; i.e. folds in which the paper lies completely flat on the table, not sticking up anywhere. This lesson allows learners to explore patterns in the number of fold lines and in their direction (i.e. mountain or valley). Thinking carefully about the interior angles of polygons enables learners to make sense of what they see.

Aims and outcomes

- Calculate the exterior angles of polygons.
- Explore patterns in flat folds.

Lesson starter (15 minutes)

Give each learner a long strip of paper. (Slicing A3 paper long-ways into strips about 5 cm in width is suitable.)

Lay the strip on the table going from left to right. Pick up the left-hand end and fold it over onto the right-hand end and crease it flat.

Now open it out and you've got a fold mark. How would you describe it?

Learners might say it is 'V'-shaped or a 'down' fold. In paper folding, they are called *valley folds* (V). Folds that stick up the other way are called *mountain folds* (M).

Now put it down again, the same way round as it was before, with the fold on the left and the open bits on the right. Now do the same folding again, left over right.

Now, before you open it, say, from left to right, what you think the folds will be like.

Most learners tend to say MVM or VMV, but there may even be disagreement over the total *number* of creases. In fact, it is MVV.

Can you explain why that happened? How do you think the pattern will develop?

Learners can explore with their paper or try to reason it out, perhaps in pairs, where there is one person to 'do' and one to 'watch'.

After the nth fold there will be $2^n - 1$ creases altogether, 2^{n-1} of which are valley folds and $2^{n-1} - 1$ of which are mountain folds (there is always one more valley than mountain). For $n > 1$, the pattern always begins with an M. The order for the first few are:

Resources for Teaching Mathematics 11–14
TEACHER SHEET

V, MVV, MMVVMVV, MMVMMVVVMMVVMVV, MMVMMVVMMMVVMVVVMMV
MMVVVMMVVMVV, . . .

To get the next pattern, take the previous one and, starting with an M at the front, interleave V then M alternately between each existing pair of letters. So to get the order for $n = 3$, for instance, start with MVV (from $n = 2$) and add m, v, m, v in between the letters given, to give mMvVmVv (the new letters are shown in lowercase).

Main lesson (25 minutes)
Give out the Task Sheets and encourage learners to follow the instructions carefully. It might be easier to demonstrate this to learners, either in small groups or with the whole class, depending on how easy they are likely to find this part.

Plenary (15 minutes)
What patterns did you find? What connections were there?

Whether a crease is a mountain or a valley depends on which side of the paper you are viewing from, so all statements about mountains and valleys should be interchangeable. The number of line segments meeting at each vertex is called the *degree (n)* of that vertex. At any vertex, let the number of mountain folds meeting there be m and the number of valley folds be v, so $n = m + v$. The difference between the number of mountain and valley folds is always 2, though which is more depends on which side of the paper you are observing from. This can be expressed as $|m - v| = 2$ or $(m - v)^2 = 4$. (This result is known as *Maekawa's theorem.*) One way to understand why this is so is to think about the angles. Imagine folding the paper back up and cutting off the tip of one of the vertices and then unfolding slightly. You would end up with a very slim polygon something like this:

Thinking about the inside of the polygon, vertices that point 'in' (concave vertices) are mountains

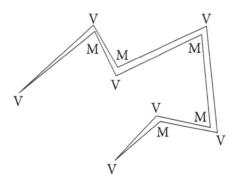

(M) and vertices that point 'out' (convex vertices) are valleys (V), as shown above. When folded up, the M angles are 360° and the V angles are 0°. Since the polygon has n sides, it must have n vertices, so its total interior angle is $180(n - 2)°$. Therefore, $180(n - 2) = 360m + 0v$, and since $n = m + v$, $180(m + v - 2) = 360m$, so $m + v - 2 = 2m$, so $v - m = 2$. Looking from the other side of the paper, we would obtain $m - v = 2$, from exactly the same argument, so in general $|m - v| = 2$, Maekawa's theorem.

Since $v = m \pm 2$ and $n = m + v$, it follows that $n = m + m \pm 2 = 2m \pm 2 = 2(m \pm 1)$, which is always even. So every vertex has an even degree: an even number of folds meeting there, as learners are likely to have noticed.

Looking at *angles*, the sum of all the angles at a vertex is clearly 360°, since it is a full turn, but the sum of *every other* angle, all the way round, is 180°. This result is known as *Kawasaki's theorem*. With a bit of imagination, this is fairly easy to prove. If the n angles, in order, around a vertex are θ_1, θ_2, θ_3, ..., θ_n, then the sum of all the angles, $\sum_{i=1}^{n} \theta_i = 360°$. (Note that n is even, since every vertex has an even degree.) When folded up, every neighbouring pair of angles correspond to a clockwise and an anticlockwise turning, which we can represent as angles of opposite signs. So $\theta_1 - \theta_2 + \theta_3 - \theta_4 + \ldots - \theta_n = 0°$, so the sum of the even-numbered angles is equal to the sum of the odd-numbered angles. Since the total is 360°, the sum of the even-numbered angles must be equal to 180°, as must be the sum of the odd-numbered angles.

Homework (5 minutes)
Learners could find out about Britney Gallivan (b. 1985) and her famous paper-folding achievement. They could also explore the 'loss function' formula $loss = \frac{1}{6}\pi d(2^n + 4)(2^n - 1)$, which gives the amount of length 'lost' when a piece of paper of thickness d is folded n times.

To make it harder
Interested learners might enjoy finding out about *dragon curves*.

To make it easier
Learners who find it difficult to make sense of what is going on could begin with just two folds and predict the mountains and valleys that they might expect to get. Unless they have done it before, when they do it and unfold the paper they are likely to be surprised that there is not an equal number of each.

Folding

Take a sheet of paper and make a flat fold in whatever direction you like.

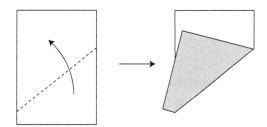

Without unfolding, make another flat fold in some other direction, however you like.

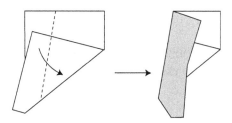

Without unfolding, make one more flat fold in some other direction.

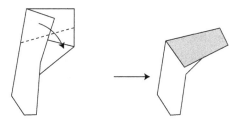

Now unfold your sheet of paper completely and look at the fold lines.
How many vertices are there, where the lines cross?

How many line segments are there?

How many line segments are there *at each vertex*?

How many line segments at each vertex are *mountain* folds? How many are *valley* folds?

What patterns can you find? Can you explain them?

Measure the *angles* at each vertex. What patterns can you find? Can you explain them?

Start with another sheet of paper and make different folds. Then unfold your sheet and investigate the patterns created.
Try to explain your results.

8

Four Numbers

Introduction

When it comes to solving equations, textbooks generally present learners with lists of arbitrary linear equations, which they are required to solve 'for practice'. In this lesson, learners generate their own practice equations by looking for equations with integer solutions. Exploring what happens when you change one equation into a slightly different equation should help learners to appreciate how the different features of an equation affect its solution.

Aims and outcomes

- Generate and solve linear equations.
- Use factors and multiples to examine when an equation will have an integer solution.

Lesson starter (15 minutes)

Write this on the board:

$$\Box x + \Box = \Box$$

Choose three numbers to go in the boxes and then solve your equation. What happens?

Did some people's choices lead to an easier job than other people's? Why?

Learners may assume that since the box symbols are the same the three numbers must be the same, which could be a useful discussion point. (In this case, there are two possibilities: if the three boxes are the same non-zero number, then $x = 0$; if the three boxes are all zero, then x can be any value.) However, you can say that the boxes do not all have to be equal to each other.

Within the possibilities suggested by learners, x may be an integer, a negative value, or perhaps any possible number (if the first box is zero and the second and third boxes are the same as each other) or zero (if the first box is not zero and the second and third boxes are the same as each other).

Try to find three box numbers that give an integer answer for x.

If $ax + b = c$, with $a \neq 0$, then $x = \frac{c - b}{a}$, so provided that a is a factor of $(c - b)$, then x will be an integer.

Main lesson (25 minutes)

Give out the Task Sheets and encourage learners to find many examples and to think about what leads to *integer* solutions.

Plenary (15 minutes)

What did you discover? Was it easy to find box numbers that gave you a particular solution for x? Why/why not?

The family of equations under study is $ax + b = cx + d$. If $a = c$ and $b = d$ (this could happen trivially if $a = b = c = d$, for instance), then the equation is an identity (and a trivial one), so any value of x will satisfy it. If $a = c$ and $b \neq d$, then the equation is self-contradictory and there are no solutions. If $a \neq c$, then $x = \frac{d - b}{a - c}$, so x will be an integer if $(a - c)$ is a factor of $(d - b)$. (If $b = d$, then $x = 0$, regardless of the values of a and c, provided they are not equal to each other.)

Interestingly, if a, b, c and d form a linear sequence (going up, or down, by the same amount each time), then $x = -1$. (See Griffiths, J. (2007) *Rich Starting Points for A-Level Core Mathematics*. Association of Teachers of Mathematics, Derby, PDF e-book, for a related situation with simultaneous equations: www.s253053503.websitehome.co.uk/articles/mydirr/simuleqs.pdf)

For $x = 3$, we need $(d - b) = 3(a - c)$; for instance, $a = 7$, $b = 11$, $c = 5$, $d = 17$.

For $\frac{a}{b}x + c = d$, we can see that b cannot be zero, and a cannot be zero unless $c = d$. Rearranging for x, we have $x = \frac{b(d - c)}{a}$, which means that x will be an integer if and only if a is a factor of $b(d - c)$.

Homework (5 minutes)

Learners could be asked to find six equations of the form $\Box x + \Box = \Box x + 3$, say, which have integer solutions, and show by solving them (or by direct argument) that the solutions are indeed integers.

To make it harder

Confident learners could extend to situations involving brackets, such as $\Box(x + \Box) = \Box x + \Box$ or introduce a division. An even harder problem would be to work on quadratics of the form $\Box x^2 + \Box = \Box x + \Box$.

To make it easier

An easier way to start would be with equations of the type $\Box x = \Box$, which have integer solutions provided that the first box number is a factor of the second. When learners are confident working on this they could add in a third box.

Four Numbers

Choose four different numbers to go in the four boxes below.

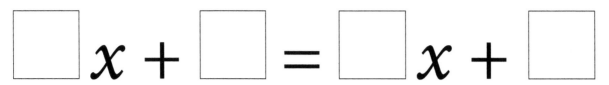

Does your equation have a solution? Why/why not?

Is the solution an integer? Why/why not?

Explore what happens with different sets of four box numbers.

Suppose you want x to be equal to 3, say, or some other number.
What different sets of four box numbers can you have now? Why?

Choose four different numbers to go in the four boxes below.

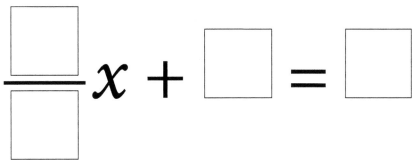

Does your equation have a solution? Why/why not?

Is the solution an integer? Why/why not?

Explore what happens with different sets of four box numbers.

9

Four Weights

Introduction

In this lesson, learners work on the 'usefulness' of different numbers in a context of addition and subtraction. Which choice of values enables the largest possible number of totals to be made? This provides many opportunities for logical thinking, as well as numerical computation. This is related to the 'stamps' problem, where you have as many as you like of two (or more) different values of stamp and the question is which total amounts can you make: see Beevers, B. S. (1994) 'Stamps', *Mathematics in School*, 29, (1), 44–5. Here, only one of each value is permitted.

There may be some confusion between the terms 'weight' and 'mass', the latter being a scalar quantity measured in, say, kilograms, the former being a vector force depending on the gravitational field strength and measured in newtons. Technically, this lesson concerns mass, but you might decide that it is easier to use the more familiar term 'weight'.

Aims and outcomes

- Solve a problem by considering all possible combinations.
- Understand and use the binary number system.

Lesson starter (10 minutes)

Here are four masses. (You could think of the units as kilograms or disregard units altogether.)

What amounts can you make by using combinations of these different masses? (You have only one of each.)

You can make all the numbers from 1 to 10.

Can you make some numbers in more than one way? Which numbers can be made in the most ways? Why?

The numbers 3, 4, 5, 6 and 7 can be made in two different ways – this table shows all possibilities.

4	3	2	1	Total	
			1	1	
		1	0	2	
		1	1	3	
	1	0	0	3	
	1	0	1	4	
	1	1	0	5	
	1	1	1	6	
1	0	0	0	4	
1	0	0	1	5	*(continued)*

4	3	2	1	Total
1	0	1	0	6
1	0	1	1	7
1	1	0	0	7
1	1	0	1	8
1	1	1	0	9
1	1	1	1	10

How can you be sure that no numbers greater than 10 are possible?

Once you have used all the masses, there are no more to use!

Main lesson (30 minutes)

What if you were allowed to change the sizes of the four masses that you had? Do you think you could get more numbers than just 1 to 10? Why/why not?

What do you think would be your best *set of four masses? Why?*

Give out the Task Sheets and encourage learners to experiment.

Plenary (15 minutes)

If you had 1, 3, 5 and 7, you could get 14 different numbers, which is an improvement on 10. You can get all the numbers from 1 to 16 (with 8 in two different ways) except for 2 and 14.

7	5	3	1	Total
			1	1
		1	0	3
		1	1	4
	1	0	0	5
	1	0	1	6
1	0	0	0	7
	1	1	0	8
1	0	0	1	8
	1	1	1	9
1	0	1	0	10
1	0	1	1	11
1	1	0	0	12
1	1	0	1	13
1	1	1	0	15
1	1	1	1	16

Will you be able to get only odd numbers, if you start with only odd masses? What if you start with all even masses?

Because odd + odd = even, it is possible to get even *or* odd numbers when starting with odd masses. But when starting with all *even* masses you can get only even numbers. (You have to have a 1 in order to get that mass.)

Do you think there is a better set? Why/why not?

The best set is 1, 2, 4 and 8. You can get all the numbers from 1 to 15, exactly once each.

8	4	2	1	Total
			1	1
		1	0	2
		1	1	3
	1	0	0	4
	1	0	1	5
	1	1	0	6
	1	1	1	7
1	0	0	0	8
1	0	0	1	9
1	0	1	0	10
1	0	1	1	11
1	1	0	0	12
1	1	0	1	13
1	1	1	0	14
1	1	1	1	15

Since there are just 15 possible combinations of the four weights ($2^n - 1$, where n is the number of masses), and we get no repeats, this must be the best solution.

With the two-pan balance, this effectively means that you have *subtraction* as well as addition. (Technically, a two-pan balance effectively compares *mass*, whereas the one-pan balance can measure only weight, although it might be *calibrated* in units of mass, assuming an appropriate gravitational field strength for the earth. You probably won't want to worry about this distinction, but a science-oriented learner might raise it!) This time, for instance, you don't need a 1, because so long as you have two masses one unit apart then you can still weigh an object to see if it has a mass of 1 unit. Now, 1, 3, 9, 27 will do all integers from 1 to 40. For more information, see Maull, M. and Porkess, R. (2000) 'Choosing Your Weights', *Mathematics in School*, 29, (1), 20–2.

Homework (5 minutes)

Imagine you had a 'broken calculator' in which everything worked except some of the buttons. Which buttons would it be best to do without? For example, could you manage without the 'times' button? Could you manage without a 'zero'? Suppose you want to be able to display all the numbers from 1 to 20, say. What is the smallest number of buttons you could do it with? Why?

For example, depending on how the calculator operates, the 'minus' button might be more useful to keep than the 'plus' button, since pressing 'minus-minus' could be the same as pressing 'plus', and so the 'minus' button alone would allow either addition or subtraction, whereas the 'plus' button wouldn't.

To make it harder

What if you have some *negative* weights (i.e. helium balloons tied to the scales that pull up the pan with a specified force)? What numbers can you make by combining 1, –2, 4 and –8, for instance? This will do every integer from 5 to –10 (except 0).

To make it easier

All learners should be able to begin by combining two masses, say, and adding them up. Careful recording might be needed to ensure that they sum every possible pair of masses.

Four Weights

You have some scales like this:

Choose four integer values for your four weights.

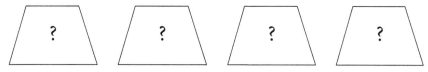

What possible amounts can you weigh with your four weights? Why?

Suppose you want to be able to weigh as many values as you can.
What do you think is the *best* set of four weights to use? Why?

Suppose instead that you have this sort of balance.

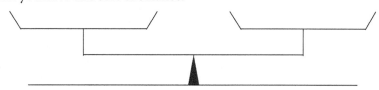

How does this make a difference?

If you could have *more than four* weights, what do you think would be the best values to choose? Why?

10

Four-Star Hotels

Introduction

This 'four-star lesson' uses grids in which each cell either contains a star or does not contain a star. The total numbers of stars for each row and column are given around the edge and the task is to use these numbers to find the locations of the stars. Learners will need to think about the number of possible solutions and reason logically through different cases.

Aims and outcomes

- Describe locations within a grid and use this to identify structure.
- Explore patterns within a grid and locate objects by following a rule.

Lesson starter (15 minutes)

Look at this:

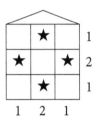

Can you see what the numbers around the edge are doing?

The edge numbers give the number of stars in that row or column. (You could include zeroes for the diagonals as well if you wanted to.)

Suppose we rub out the stars. Is there anywhere else we can put the stars so that all the edge numbers still tell the truth? Why/why not?

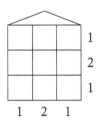

There are in fact four other possible arrangements that satisfy the same edge numbers.

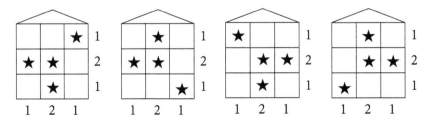

How can you be sure that there are no more possibilities?

Learners should be able to justify why they know that they have considered all possible arrangements. One way is to begin with the middle row (or column) and consider the three possible ways of putting two stars into it. For one of these (star at the top and star at the bottom), there is only one possible position for the final two stars that satisfies the numbers around the edge; for the other two there are two ways each, giving a total of five arrangements altogether.

Main lesson (25 minutes)

Suppose that you just have the edge numbers. *What do the edge numbers* (a, b, c, d, e, f, *below) tell you about the location of the stars in the grid? Why?*

Can you tell from the numbers how many stars there are altogether? How? Can you tell where they are located? Why/why not?

?	?	?	*d*
?	?	?	*e*
?	?	?	*f*
a	*b*	*c*	

Give out the Task Sheet and encourage learners to investigate the different possibilities, initially with exactly four stars and then, perhaps, with different numbers of stars.

Plenary (15 minutes)

How many possible star placements are there for any particular six edge numbers? Why?

How many possible edge numbers are there for any particular total number of stars? Why?

Did you find one of these questions easier to answer than the other? Why/why not?

The horizontal edge numbers (a, b, c) and the vertical edge numbers (d, e, f) are partitions of 4 into 3. In other words, $a + b + c = 4$ and $d + e + f = 4$, and each of a, b, c, d, e and f are integers between 0 and 3 inclusive. The only possible triplets satisfying these conditions are: (0, 1, 3), (0, 2, 2) and (1, 1, 2), in any orderings.

If you have (0, 1, 3) along the bottom edge, say, then one column contains 3 stars, meaning that every row contains at least one star, so the right edge must be (≥ 1, ≥ 1, ≥ 1), ruling out both (0, 1, 3) and (0, 2, 2). So (0, 1, 3) has to go with (1, 1, 2) in some order.

For *three stars*, the triplets must be (0, 0, 3) and (1, 1, 1), or (0, 1, 2) and (1, 1, 1), or (0, 1, 2) and (0, 1, 2), or (1, 1, 1) and (1, 1, 1), if the stars lie along a diagonal. (*Six stars* is just the reverse of this.)

For *two stars*, the triplets must be (0, 1, 1) and (0, 0, 2) or (0, 1, 1) and (0, 1, 1). (*Seven stars* is just the reverse of this.)

For *one star*, the triplets must, of course, be (0, 0, 1) both ways. (*Eight stars* is just the reverse of this.)

There are connections here to solving simultaneous equations, where in general as many mutually independent pieces of information are needed as there are unknowns to find.

Homework (5 minutes)

An easier version to explore completely for homework would be the two-by-two case, in which it is much easier to locate the positions of the stars.

Does every possible set of four numbers around the edge correspond to exactly one *arrangement of stars? Why/why not?*

The answer is no, but only just! There are $2^4 = 16$ possible 2×2 hotels (using up to four stars), since each cell can either contain a star or not contain a star. Writing the numbers around the edge as (a, b, c, d), as shown below, there are 15 possible sets of edge numbers, so one ambiguous case (1, 1, 1, 1), for which there are two possibilities (shown shaded below).

The possible edge numbers (a, b, c, d) and the grids are listed below.

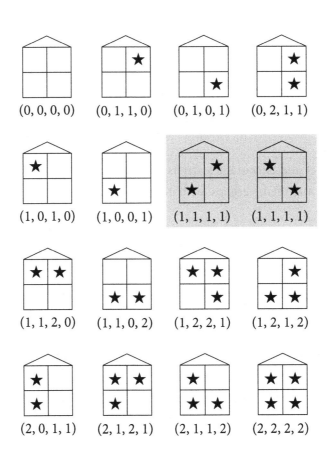

To make it harder

Keen learners could investigate what happens with *five* stars. In fact, this is closely connected to the four-star situation, since there are nine squares altogether. Imagine that every square that does not contain a star contains a circle, say, and delete all the stars (if you wish). The numbers around the edge can each be subtracted from nine to give the numbers of circles. So we can generate a five-circle grid from every four-star grid. So the number of possible grids will be exactly the same for five stars as for four stars. They are equivalent.

To make it easier

Learners who have difficulty beginning could examine what happens with just two stars, where the numbers around the edge can be only 0, 1 or 2. An enlarged photocopy of the 'hotel' and two plastic counters might also be helpful.

Four-Star Hotels

Place four stars ★ ★ ★ ★ into each of the 'hotels' below, writing around the edges the numbers in each row and column.

What numbers are possible around the edge? Why?

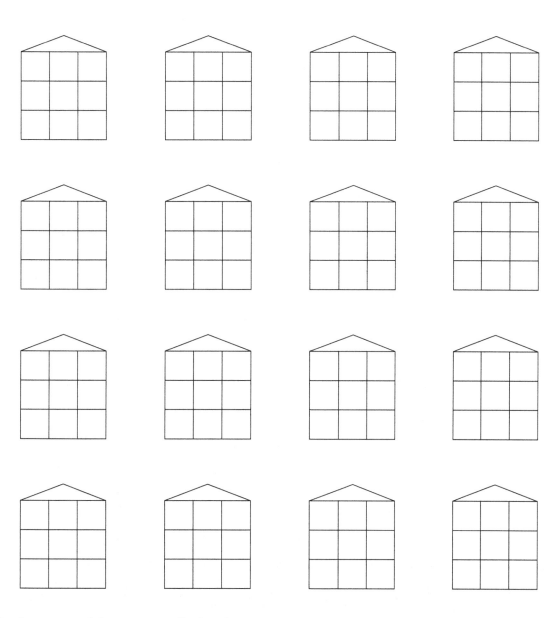

What happens with bigger or smaller hotels?

What happens with more or fewer stars?

11

Fuel

Introduction

'Doing the impossible' can often make for an interesting puzzle or investigation. In this lesson, learners work on trying to transfer fuel across a desert that initially seems too wide to get across. By stockpiling fuel along the way, it becomes possible to cover much larger distances. There are many opportunities for learners to use logical thinking and develop strategies for solving the problem.

Aims and outcomes

- Develop a mathematical model for a pseudo-real-life problem.
- Solve a maximization/minimization problem.

Lesson starter (10 minutes)

Suppose you are driving a very fuel-inefficient van that consumes 1 litre of fuel for every 1 km you travel. How far can you get on 75 litres of fuel (a full tank)? What if you want to get home again?

You could get 75 km from the starting point, or $\frac{75}{2}$ = 35.5 km, if you wanted to save enough fuel to return. You could envisage this as a region bounded by a circle of radius 37.5 km, centred on the starting point. (Of course, in reality maybe the tank would have a bit of reserve at the bottom, or perhaps the engine wouldn't run right down to the very last drop of fuel.)

How could you get further than this? Suppose you are in a desert.

Obviously getting the van fixed, or switching it for one with a bigger tank, or taking bottles of fuel, or stopping to refuel along the way are possibilities. As these are suggested, you could gently rule them out: 'There are no petrol stations in this desert.'

Someone may suggest going backwards and forwards to a spot 10 km away, say, and dumping fuel there. It will take only 20 litres of fuel to get there and back, so you could dump 55 litres there every time until you have a stockpile. Then that could be your 'starting point'. If no one suggests anything, move on to the main lesson anyway.

Main lesson (30 minutes)

Give out the Task Sheets and encourage learners to work on the problem, perhaps making a sketch (or scale drawing) to indicate what positions can be reached by what strategies. There is a lot of scope for learners to experiment and investigate the effect of changing the numbers.

Plenary (15 minutes)

How much fuel did you manage to get across? How much did you 'waste'?

Did anyone do better? How did you do it?

The answer is 60 litres. Since the van can take a maximum of 75 litres each time it leaves the starting point, in order to remove all of the 200 litres it will need to leave $\left\lceil \frac{200}{75} \right\rceil$ = 3 times (where the brackets indicate the ceiling function – rounding up to the nearest integer). So the van will make three outbound trips and two returns during the first leg of the journey. Provided the distance to the first dumping spot is less than $\frac{75}{2}$ = 35.5 km away, it will be able to get back to collect more fuel. Suppose that the distance to this first dumping spot is x km. From here, it will make two outward trips and one return, through a distance y km to the second dumping spot, from which it will make one trip out to the far side of the dessert, a further distance z km.

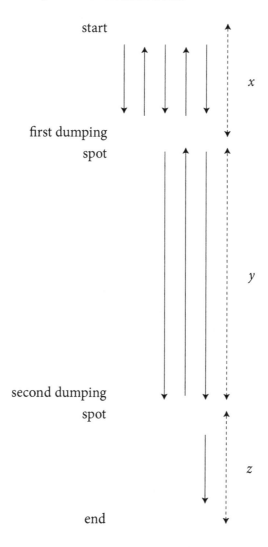

The first leg of the journey consumes $5x$ litres of fuel (since 5 trips of distance x are made), the second leg of the journey consumes $3y$ litres of fuel and the final leg consumes z litres. The situation will be optimal if we dump a total of exactly 2×75 litres at the first dumping spot and exactly 1×75 litres at the second dumping spot. This will happen if $200 - 5x = 150$ and $150 - 3y = 75$, giving $x = 10$ km and $y = 25$ km. Since the total journey is 50 km, this means that $z = 50 - 10 - 25 = 15$ km. Starting out with 75 litres at the second dumping spot means that by the time we reach the end we will have $75 - z = 60$ litres of fuel remaining. Learners may not make such a detailed and generalized analysis, but may obtain similar answers by trial and improvement.

Homework (5 minutes)

Make up another puzzle like this. Perhaps have people at both ends of the desert, trying to meet somewhere in between. If their vans have different fuel efficiencies (or different tank sizes), where is the most sensible place to meet? Why?

To make it harder

Suppose the van has to return to the starting point afterwards. If it needs enough fuel to get back, what effect will this have on the solution? Why?

To make it easier

Using counters or cubes, or drawing a graph, to represent the amount of fuel still present at each stage could help learners who find it hard to begin.

Fuel

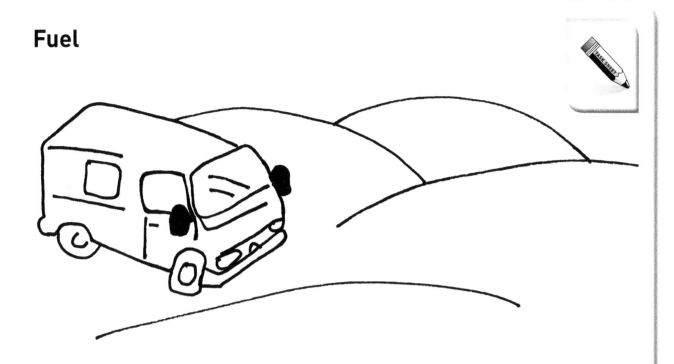

- A van has to transport fuel across a 50 km stretch of desert.
- The van can carry a maximum of 75 litres of fuel at any one time.
- The van is extremely fuel-inefficient. It uses up 1 litre of fuel for every 1 km it travels.

If 200 litres of fuel is available at the start, how much do you think it is possible to get to the other side of the desert? Why?

How do you do it?

Can you be sure that this is the best solution possible? Why/why not?

Make up other problems like this one.

12

Have a Megaday!

Introduction

There is much potential confusion associated with our complicated systems of time and date units, which have developed gradually, for historical reasons rather than because they are particularly easy to use. There have been many attempts to apply the metric system to these measures since *French Revolutionary Time* was introduced in 1793, which divided up the day into 10 hours, each hour into 100 minutes and each minute into 100 seconds. But they have not caught on. Learners are sometimes unsure whether 'a day' is 24 hours or 12 hours ('If a 'day' is 24 hours, how long is a 'night'?'). This lesson looks at some problems to do with time. If you have the opportunity, it would be nice to do this work on a date with some interesting significance; e.g. a Friday 13th or the first of a month, or 16 September (100 days to Christmas).

Aims and outcomes

- Convert time units confidently.
- Understand and use common metric prefixes.

Lesson starter (10 minutes)

Do you think today's date is 'special' in any way? If so, why? When will something like this next happen? Why? If not, when do you think the next 'special' date is and why?

See what ideas learners have. They might be personal, relating to their birthday or some event in their family life. Dates may be religiously or culturally significant. If there appears to be nothing special, you could calculate the number of days until various special dates in the future.

Main lesson (30 minutes)

Today we are going to think about some made-up names for amounts of time. I want you to try to work out what they mean. The first one is 'megaday'.

A 'megaday' sounds good, but how long do you think a 'megaday' is? Why?

'Mega' is a standard prefix meaning 'million', so a megaday is 1 000 000 days, which is about 2700 years.

What about a kiloday, a centiday, a milliday, a microday, and any more that you can think of? Where will you be in a centiday or in a kiloday? Why?

1 kiloday = 1000 days = about 2.7 years or 2 years 270 days.

$$1 \text{ centiday} = \frac{1}{100} \text{ day} = \frac{24}{100} \text{ hours} = 0.24 \text{ hours} = 14.4 \text{ minutes} = 14 \text{ minutes } 24 \text{ seconds.}$$

$$1 \text{ milliday} = \frac{1}{1000} \text{ day} = \frac{24}{1000} \text{ hours} = 0.024 \text{ hours} = 1.44 \text{ minutes} = 1 \text{ minute } 26.4 \text{ seconds.}$$

$$1 \text{ microday} = \frac{1}{1\,000\,000} \text{ day} = \frac{24}{1\,000\,000} \text{ hours} = 86.4 \text{ milliseconds.}$$

What other units like this can you invent and convert?

Learners may suggest microyears (about 32 seconds), millicenturies (about 37 days), microdecades (about 5 minutes – 'I'll be with you in a microdecade!' – it could catch on?), etc.

Give out the Task Sheets and encourage learners to work on how long after today various times will have been reached.

Plenary (15 minutes)

What units did you invent? How did you work out how long they were? Who else did that one? Do you agree? Why/why not?

Values are given below, correct to 2 significant figures where necessary.

	Century	Decade	Year	Month	Fortnight
Giga-	10^{11} years	10^{10} years	10^9 years	8.3×10^7 years	3.8×10^7 years
Mega-	10^8 years	10^7 years	10^6 years	8.3×10^4 years	3.8×10^4 years
Kilo-	10^5 years	10^4 years	1000 years	83 years	38 years
Centi-	1 year	37 days	3.7 days	7.4 hours	3.4 hours
Milli-	37 days	3.7 days	8.8 hours	45 minutes	20 minutes
Micro-	53 minutes	5.3 minutes	32 seconds	2.7 seconds	1.2 seconds
	Week	**Day**	**Hour**	**Minute**	**Second**
Giga-	1.9×10^7 years	2.7×10^6 years	1.1×10^5 years	1900 years	32 years
Mega-	1.9×10^4 years	2700 years	110 years	1.9 years	1.6 weeks
Kilo-	19 years	2.7 years	42 days	17 hours	17 minutes
Centi-	1.7 hours	14 minutes	36 seconds	0.6 seconds	10 milliseconds
Milli-	10 minutes	1.4 minutes	3.6 seconds	60 milliseconds	1 millisecond
Micro-	0.60 seconds	86 milliseconds	3.6 milliseconds	60 microseconds	1 microsecond

Homework (5 minutes)

When will it be a kilohour to your birthday? Explain how you worked it out.

The answer will be 42 days before their birthday.

To make it harder

There are many date-related problems that confident learners could work on. For example, *How many Friday 13ths are there this year? Will there be the same number every year? Why/why not?*

There is always at least one and there are never more than three. The easiest way to think about it is to calculate 'modulus 7'. Learners could try to see how this table helps:

Month	Jan	Feb	Mar	Apr	May	Jun	Jul	Aug	Sep	Oct	Nov	Dec
Remainder (mod 7)	3	0	3	2	3	2	3	3	2	3	2	3

(February would be 1 in a leap year, because 29 = 1 mod 7.) For more information, see Wyvill, R. (1973) 'Friday the Thirteenth', *Mathematics in School*, 2, (4), 29.

To make it easier

Learners who find this hard could benefit from writing down each stage and perhaps starting by creating a conversion chart such as the following:

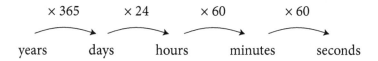

Sometimes learners think that the arrows are going the wrong way, because a day is *longer* than a hour, so why are you multiplying? But if you have 2 days then because there are 24 hours in each then there will be 48 hours, which is 2 × 24.

Have a Megaday!

Make up some units by combining a prefix on the left with a time unit on the right.
If you can think of other possibilities, include those as well.

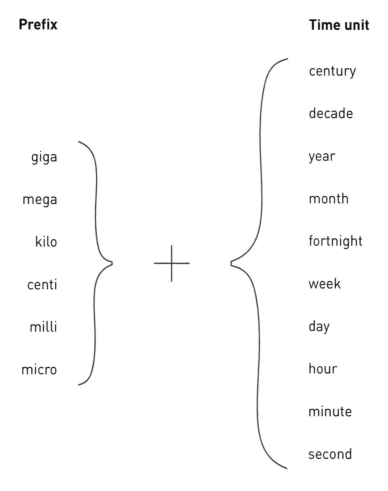

Prefix		Time unit
		century
		decade
giga		year
mega		month
kilo	+	fortnight
centi		week
milli		day
micro		hour
		minute
		second

You could also use units like these, if you can decide how long you think they are:

lifetime, afternoon, meal-time, night, eye-blink

About how long do you think these units should be? Why?

Make up questions like this:

Which is longer: a mega-eye-blink or a micro-lifetime?

Make sure you can justify your answers!

13

How Far?

Introduction

Some people say that as the world gets smaller people actually think it is bigger than it is, and tend to overestimate distances to 'far away' places. In surveys, people frequently overestimate distances to places in other countries; for example, Londoners thinking that Paris is further from London than Newcastle is. In this lesson, learners devise an experiment to test statistical hypotheses concerning people's estimates of distances.

Aims and outcomes

- Design and carry out a survey to test a statistical hypothesis.
- Estimate distances on the surface of the earth.

Lesson starter (15 minutes)

Individually, without conferring with anyone else, write down in miles how far away you think these places are from here. Don't worry about trying to work it out exactly – just put down your best guesses.

(Choose a couple of well-known cities, one nearby and one further away. Then choose the capital cities of some nearby countries and some further afield. If you have the internet available [search for 'distance calculator'], you could check some of these 'live' when learners reveal their estimates). Learners may be a long way out with some. Are their answers even in the correct *order*?

Are there any patterns to the ones we were more accurate or less accurate about? Why do you think that might be?

Main lesson (25 minutes)

Give out the Task Sheets. Learners could discuss and plan in groups and then write their questionnaires. They will need access to the internet or to atlases or tables in order to find the true distances.

Plenary (15 minutes)

What points did you think were important? What ideas did you have?

Learners may consider points such as the following.

- Has the person been there – on holiday, perhaps?
- Will older people have more experience of places, or perhaps do younger people travel more widely?
- What if someone was born in a different country? Might that help or hinder?
- Should we check to see if they have studied or are interested in geography?
- Might some occupations give an advantage, e.g. an aeroplane pilot?
- How accurate will people have to be to count as 'correct'? Will you give them a multiple choice of several distances? How will you make sure that your options don't give the correct answer away (e.g. always having the correct answer as the middle one)?

There is much for learners to think about and discuss.

Do you think that people estimate vertical distances differently from horizontal ones? Why/why not?

There is an argument from evolution that large vertical drops are so dangerous that we have a survival advantage if we overestimate them and are correspondingly over-cautious about them. For more information, see Jackson, R. E. and Cormack, L. K. (2007) 'Evolved Navigation Theory and the Descent Illusion', *Perception & Psychophysics*, 69, (3), 353–62.

Homework (5 minutes)

Carry out the survey, perhaps among friends and family. (You might want to remind learners not to approach strangers unless they have an adult who will accompany them.)

To make it harder

Confident learners could consider the following.

Why do different sources give slightly different values for the distance from London to New York, for example? Find out about 'fractals' and the problems in defining the length of a river. Find out why there are different answers to the question 'Which is the tallest mountain in the world?'

Defining the source of a river can be problematic (e.g. the Nile), and the wiggly nature (*sinuosity*) of many rivers means that the more finely you carry out your measurements the greater the value you will get for the length. Also, rivers can change significantly with the seasons and depending on the amount of recent rain. Learners could find out about the disagreement over whether the Nile or the Amazon is the longest river in the world. The height of a mountain is customarily measured above sea level, but visually a mountain appears higher if it is higher relative to the surrounding land. If you measured from the centre of the earth then, because of the 'bulge' of the earth at the equator (the earth is more of an *oblate spheroid* than a sphere), you would obtain completely different answers. And it can be hard to measure relative to sea level if the sea is a long way away from the mountain.

Many people have a fairly accurate idea of how many hours it takes to fly to various places. Can you construct a chart to allow conversion of flight time into approximate distance?

The average speed of a modern jet aeroplane could be taken as 500 miles per hour.

Find out about 'spherical geometry' and how you can have a triangle with three right angles on the surface of the earth.

If an aeroplane flies south from the North Pole until it gets to the equator, turns left 90°, flies one quarter of the way around the world, along the equator, turns left 90° and flies back up to the North Pole, it has traced out a spherical triangle containing three right angles. The angle sum of any triangle drawn on a sphere is more than 180° – the larger the triangle, the bigger the angle sum.

To make it easier

Learners who have great difficulty estimating distances could examine an atlas and consider the different scales on the page, or use Google Earth and look carefully at the scale at each stage.

How Far?

Do you think that people are generally good at estimating distances? Why/why not?

What might make one place easier for someone to estimate the distance to than another?

What might make someone better at estimating distances generally?

Try to think of some hypotheses that you could test with a survey.

What questions will you ask?

Who will you ask?

How will you ask them?

14

Infinity

Introduction

This lesson provides an opportunity for learners to explore the idea of a sequence that converges, perhaps even making and solving quadratic equations to find the limit. Every time learners see a decimal expansion such as $\frac{1}{3} = 0.3333333\ldots$ they are effectively encountering infinity, since we can think of this fraction as an infinite geometric progression: $\frac{1}{3} = \frac{3}{10} + \frac{3}{100} + \frac{3}{1000} + \frac{3}{10\,000}$. Doing the division 'by hand' may convince learners that the 'remainder 1' is always going to appear and that therefore the process will go on forever.

Aims and outcomes

- Form and solve quadratic equations.
- Investigate the convergence of sequences.

Lesson starter (15 minutes)

You need some paper suitable for tearing up – an unwanted official document would be ideal!

Take a sheet of paper and tear it in half. Put one piece down and tear the other piece in half. Put one piece down and tear the other piece in half. Carry on. What happens?

What will eventually happen?

However many times you do it, there will always be a small bit of paper in your hand, but you can get as much of the paper down on the table as you like by doing enough steps. Eventually, all the paper will be in the heap, but this will take infinitely many steps. This suggests that $\frac{1}{2} + \frac{1}{4} + \frac{1}{8} + \frac{1}{16} = 1$, provided that the '$+ \ldots$' means including every subsequent term forever. This sequence is *convergent*.

What do you think will happen with thirds?

Take another sheet of paper and tear it into thirds. Put one piece down on the left, another piece down on the right and keep the third piece in your hand. Tear this piece into thirds. Put one piece down on the left, another piece down on the right and keep the third piece in your hand. Carry on. What happens?

This time you will eventually end up with two identical piles of paper, each equal to half of the paper you started with, suggesting that $\frac{1}{3} + \frac{1}{9} + \frac{1}{27} + \frac{1}{81} + \ldots = \frac{1}{2}$. In general, $\frac{1}{n} + \frac{1}{n^2} + \frac{1}{n^3} + \frac{1}{n^4} + \ldots = \frac{1}{n-1}$, provided that $n > 1$.

Main lesson (25 minutes)

Give out the Task Sheets. Learners could explore the process using spreadsheets or calculators. Encourage them to record what is happening as they go.

Plenary (15 minutes)

What happened? Did it depend on the starting number? How? What other things did you try? What did you find out?

If the process converges to a value x, then $\sqrt{x} + 6 = x$, which means that $\sqrt{x} = x - 6$, so $x = x^2 - 12x + 36$, so $x^2 - 13x + 36 = 0$, giving $(x - 9)(x - 4)$, so $x = 9$ or 4.

Resources for Teaching Mathematics 11–14
TEACHER SHEET

For what starting values will the process converge? Will it converge to 9 or to 4. Why?

Plotting the graphs $y = \sqrt{x} + 6$ and $y = x$ on the same axes shows that they cross at $(9, 9)$, and since the $y = \sqrt{x} + 6$ graph is shallow near the solution it should converge to 9 for all positive values of x. Convergence is fast: even beginning with 100, the solution is reached, correct to 3 significant figures, in only five iterations. (We cannot get the $x = 4$ solution, since it comes from overlap of the $y = x$ graph with the $y = -\sqrt{x} + 6$ graph, which does not appear, since we are taking *positive* square roots.)

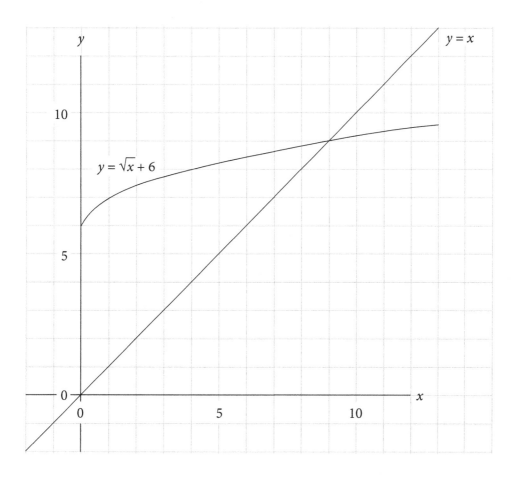

In general, if the 'Add 6' stage is 'Add a', where $a > 0$, then if the process converges, it will converge to a solution of the equation $\sqrt{x} + a = x$, giving $x^2 - (2a + 1)x + a^2 = 0$. This will have real solutions only if $(2a + 1)^2 - 4a^2 \geq 0$; i.e. if $4a + 1 \geq 0$, which is guaranteed, if $a > 0$. If $4a + 1$ is a perfect square (as it was in the original case, where $a = 6$ and $4a + 1 = 25$), then the solutions will be integers. All odd squares are of the form $4a + 1$, where a is an integer, so provided that a is twice a triangle number, we will obtain an integer solution. So we can have $a = 2, 6, 12, 20, \ldots$ and the solution will always be $x = \frac{2a + 1 + \sqrt{4a + 1}}{2}$. When $a = 6$, this gives $\frac{2(6) + 1 + \sqrt{4(6) + 1}}{2} = \frac{12 + 1 + 5}{2} = 9$, as seen above.

Homework (5 minutes)

Learners could find out about the *Collatz conjecture*, a very easy-to-understand idea, yet still an unsolved problem in mathematics.

To make it harder

Confident learners could try replacing 'square root' with 'cube root' or taking the *negative* square root.

To make it easier

Learners who find it hard to keep track of what is going on might benefit from recording the number obtained in each stage in a table. They could also use spreadsheet software to do the number crunching, allowing them to focus all their attention on what is happening to the values.

Infinity

Try putting numbers into this flow diagram.

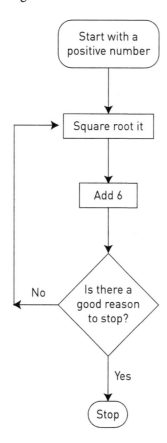

What happens with different numbers? Why?

What if you change 'Add 6' to something else?

When do you get *convergence*? Why?

When do you get *convergence to an integer*? Why?

Find out as much as you can about processes like these.

15

Investigating Mirrors

Introduction

Mirrors are a common feature in everyday life but they can seem like mysterious things. They fascinate babies from an early age, and looking at yourself in a curved mirror can be amusing. There is a clip on the internet (search www.youtube.com for 'mirror, prank, washroom' – but make sure you check all the way through any clips beforehand to ensure suitability) in which a public washroom is set up with a large glass wall instead of a mirror and twins on each side, mirroring each other's movements, but anyone else who enters the washroom is bamboozled by not seeing *their* reflection in the mirror. It is clearly a highly disorientating experience not to see your reflection when you expect to, and learners will enjoy watching this short clip if you have time. In this lesson, learners examine the effect of reflections of an object in more than one mirror.

Aims and outcomes

- Describe one transformation in terms of others.
- Explore the effect of multiple reflections on a shape.

Lesson starter (10 minutes)

What happens when you reflect something in a mirror? Can you describe it in words?

The object is 'turned around' or 'flipped over'. Learners may disagree about whether it is turned around 'vertically' or 'horizontally', leading to the common conundrum that asks why mirrors swap left to right (your right side becomes your left side and your left side becomes your right side) but not up to down (your head doesn't end up on the floor and your feet at the top!). You could see if they can work out why.

What if you reflect it twice?

Learners may say that you 'get back to where you started'.

Has anything changed? What if it isn't in the same *mirror?*

Unless both reflections take place in the same mirror, the *position* will have changed.

What happens if you stand in between two parallel mirrors? What do you see? (E.g. in a bathroom.)

You see infinitely many copies of yourself stretching off into the distance both ways!

How far apart are your first images in front and behind?

They are twice the separation of the mirrors (or the length of the room).

Main lesson (30 minutes)

Give out the Task Sheets and encourage learners to experiment and see what happens. Some small mirrors might be helpful.

Plenary (15 minutes)

You might want to have several plenaries, depending on how far different learners have got at different times.

What do you think happens? Why?

A schematic drawing helps:

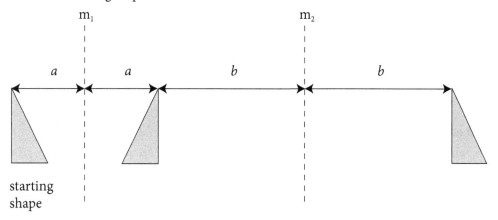

The overall transformation is a translation to the right by a distance equal to twice the distance between the mirrors and in a direction perpendicular to them.

What if you reflect first in m_2 and then in m_1?

The result is that this time the triangle moves the same amount but to the *left*.

If the mirrors are *non*-parallel, at an angle θ to one another ($\theta < 180°$), then the result of reflecting first in m_1 and then in m_2 is to rotate the shape by an angle of 2θ in the same sense as m_2 is from m_1.

Homework (5 minutes)

Find out what a kaleidoscope is and how it works. How would you go about making one?

What do you think are the best angles to have between the mirrors? Why?

A similar, and interesting, device is the less-well-known teleidoscope.

Find out about 'mirroring' in body language and look out for it in daily life or on television. Be ready to report back on examples.

To make it harder

Confident learners might like to consider the following question:

How long does a full-length mirror need to be? Does it need to be 6 feet tall to cater for a 6-foot tall person? Why/why not?

In fact it needs only to be *half* your height.

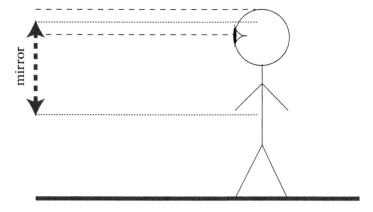

If the mirror is positioned with its top halfway between the eyeline and the level of the top of the head, and with its bottom halfway between the eyeline and the ground, then all parts from head to toe will be visible and the mirror will have exactly half the length of the person. Notice that it doesn't depend on how far away from the mirror you stand. Drawing in some rays will help. To cater for people of different heights, a slightly longer mirror will be needed, otherwise you would need to adjust the height for each person using it.

Why then do people stand close to a mirror if they want to see better?

You can see more *detail* up close, but not a greater proportion of the body. Obviously this will not be quite true if you lean over towards the mirror.

To make it easier
Learners who find this difficult might benefit from using some small actual mirrors to explore what is happening.

Investigating Mirrors

Reflect the triangle in mirror line m_1.
Then reflect the *image* in the *other* mirror line, m_2.

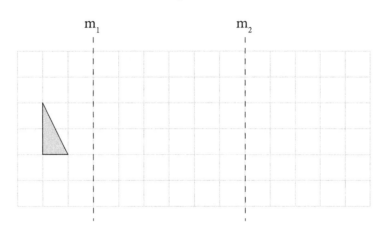

What transformation is equivalent to the *combined* effect of these *two* reflections?

Try moving the starting triangle to different positions. What happens?
What if the triangle starts *in between* the mirrors? What if it starts *to the right* of m_2?

Try moving the mirrors to different distances apart. What happens? Why?
Try to summarize all the possibilities.

What happens if the mirrors are *not* parallel to each other? Why?

What happens if there are more than two mirrors? Why?

16

Journey Through a Word

Introduction

Sometimes it can be interesting to see what happens if you deliberately make something harder than it need be. Using the 'wrong tools' for the job can lead to useful thought. This lesson avoids describing a journey by coordinates (which would be easy, in this case) and instead insists on using distances and bearings (which is much harder).

Aims and outcomes

- Create a coded message using letters positioned in a grid.
- Use distances and bearings to describe positions.

Lesson starter (15 minutes)

Do some mental imagery. If learners find this too hard, you could initially have some axes drawn on the board to refer to, but you could try rubbing out at least part of them as you go on, or deliberately using numbers off the scales at times.

Imagine some axes and suppose that the positive y-axis is north.

What is the bearing of (3, 2) from (2, 2)? Why?

It is 090°, because it is due east.

What is the bearing of (2, 2) from (3, 2)? Why?

It is 270°, because it is due west.

What other questions like this can you ask that don't involve us in measuring or doing trigonometry?

Which points are on a bearing of 045 ° from (3, 1)?

All points on the *half-line* $y = x - 2$, $x > 3$. Points on the other half, $y = x - 2$, $x < 3$ would have a bearing of $180 + 45 = 225°$. When $x = 3$, the bearing of (3, 1) from itself is not defined.

Can you find a connection between the equation of a straight-line graph and the bearing of one point on the line from another point on the line?

The bearing of one point from another (with smaller x value) on the line $y = mx + c$ will be $90 - \tan^{-1}m$, provided that $m > 0$. Keen learners could consider other cases.

Main lesson (25 minutes)

Give out the Task Sheets.

Imagine life without coordinates! You have to describe routes around the letters and symbols using bearings and distances only.

For example, the word MATHS would be:

037°, 5.0 units (origin to M)

315°, 2.8 units (M to A)

127°, 5.0 units (A to T)

315°, 2.8 units (T to H – the same vector as M to A)

153°, 2.2 units (H to S)

Learners will need to be quite accurate for it to work, and once you go wrong, you will find that you get gibberish from then on! (Repeated letters can be awkward, so just say 'stay' if you want the same letter again.)

Plenary (15 minutes)

(A spreadsheet is available that will instantly calculate the bearing of any pair of coordinates from any other.)

What messages did you make? Were some easier to do than others?

Are there any that you can do without a protractor?

Learners who don't have their protractors can still work out angles for routes based on 45°, 90°, 180°, etc. For example, 'COOL GAME' would be a possible message utilizing this self-imposed handicap.

Homework (5 minutes)

Invent another coordinate system, i.e. another way of describing position or journeys in two or three dimensions. *How could you extend bearings to positions in* three *dimensions?*

Keen learners could find out about *polar, cylindrical* and *spherical* coordinates systems.

To make it harder

Confident learners could try to find a rule for converting two pairs of coordinates into the bearing of the second pair from the first, and the first pair from the second. They could try writing a formula for a spreadsheet program to calculate this.

If the *x* and *y* coordinates of the first and second points are in cells (C2, E2), (I2, K2) of the spreadsheet, then a formula such as

```
=IF(C2-I2=0,IF(E2>K2,0,180),IF(C2-I2>0,90-(180/PI()*ATAN((E2-K2)/
(C2-I2))),270-(180/PI()*ATAN((E2-K2)/(C2-I2)))))
```

will give the bearing of the first point from the second, even in 'difficult' cases such as when one point is directly due north or south of the other.

To make it easier

Learners who find this hard could begin using bearings between 000° and 180° only and see what words they can make under that constraint, e.g. MINT. When they are comfortable working up to 180° they could extend to larger angles.

Coordinates Are Banned!

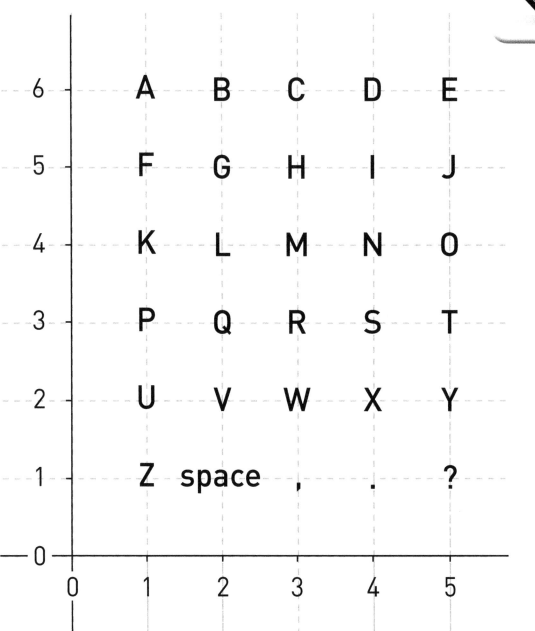

© Colin Foster (2011) *Resources for Teaching Mathematics 11–14*. London: Continuum

Make up a message using the letters and punctuation marks above.

Use bearings and distances to describe the route around your message, starting at the origin (0, 0).

For repeated letters, just say 'stay'.

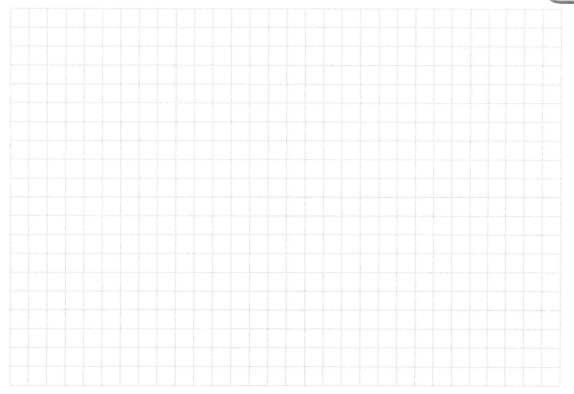

Give your instructions to someone else. Can they decode your message?

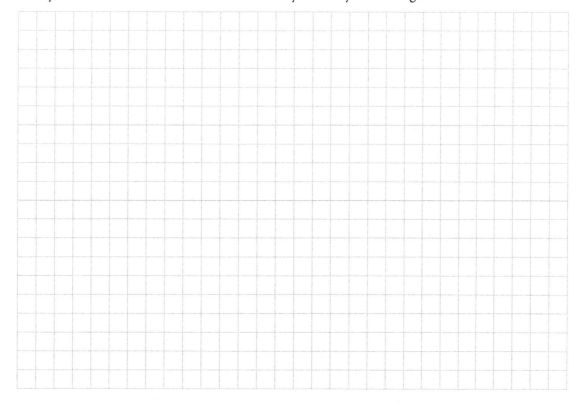

17

Ladders

Introduction

There is a long tradition of pseudo-real-life ladder problems in mathematics lessons. Some of these are very hard, such as the classic one in which a ladder leans against a cube resting against a wall (see www.mathematische-basteleien.de/ladder.htm). The task used in this lesson is much more straightforward, giving an opportunity for working on simultaneous linear equations.

Aims and outcomes

- Draw and interpret straight-line graphs.
- Solve pairs of simultaneous linear equations.

Lesson starter (10 minutes)

Suppose that the y-axis represents a wall and the x-axis represents the floor. Let's have another wall at x = 10. Can you picture this in your mind?

Tell us the equation of a line that could represent a ladder resting with its foot at the left wall. Maybe try to think of several. What is the same about them all?

Any equation of the form $y = mx$, where $m > 0$, will do.

Find an equation of a line that could be a ladder resting with its foot at the right *wall.*

Maybe try to think of several. What is the same about them all?

This is harder than before, because the constraint now, instead of being that the x- and y-intercepts are zero, is that the x-intercept is 10. Solutions now are lines of the form $y = k(10 - x)$, where $k > 0$. Learners may not express this algebraically, but possible examples could be collected on the board and patterns conjectured. Alternatively, they might think of it as $x = ny + 10$, where $n < 0$. (Clearly, the ladder, unlike a mathematical line, is of finite length, so the ladder is represented by only a *segment* of the entire line.)

Main lesson (30 minutes)

Now choose one of the left-wall ladders and one of the right-wall ladders to work on. We are going to think about where they cross.

Give out the Task Sheets and encourage learners to consider where their ladders will cross.

Learners may think the ladders will prop each other up, but we are imagining that they are not in the same plane, and therefore, when viewed from the side, they will *appear* to intersect without actually touching.

Plenary (15 minutes)

What integer crossing points did you manage to find ladders for?

In general, the lines $y = mx$, with $m > 0$, and $y = k(10 - x)$, with $k > 0$, will cross at $\left(\dfrac{10k}{k + m}, \dfrac{10km}{k + m} \right)$. For integer m and k, the coordinates will also both be integers provided that $k + m$ is a factor of $10k$. Learners may notice (perhaps in simple cases, not necessarily in the generalized way stated here) that since the left-hand ladder hits the right-hand wall at $(10, 10m)$ and the right-hand ladder hits the left-hand wall at $(0, 10k)$, the height of the crossing point, $\dfrac{10km}{k + m}$, is the *harmonic mean* of $10m$ and $10k$, since $\dfrac{1}{\left(\dfrac{10km}{k + m} \right)} = \dfrac{1}{10k} + \dfrac{1}{10m}$, which can be also be seen by using similar triangles.

For any given intersection point (a, b), with $0 < a < 10$ and $b > 0$, there will be only one possible pair of ladders that will intersect there, given by the equations $y = \dfrac{bx}{a}$ and $y = \dfrac{b(10 - x)}{10 - a}$, so, for instance, given the point $(3, 4)$, the two ladders must be $y = \dfrac{4x}{3}$ and $y = \dfrac{4(10 - x)}{7}$.

Homework (5 minutes)

Find out about other mathematical 'ladder problems' and bring in one that you understand and can explain.

To make it harder

Confident learners could fix one of the ladders and try to find a series of possible second ladders which lead to intersection points at all the integer x coordinates from 1 to 9. What patterns do they find in their equations?

To make it easier

Learners having difficulty could begin by having one ladder reach twice as far up the wall as the other. Graph-drawing software (or someone with a graphical calculator) could help with finding suitable equations and checking the intersection points.

Ladders

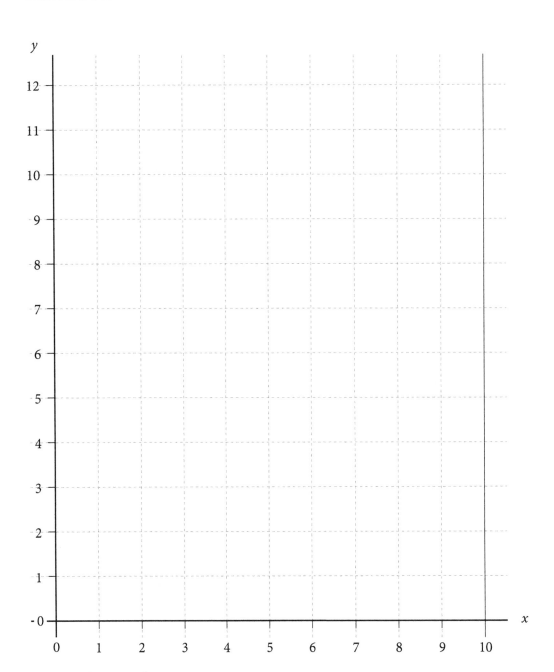

Choose the equations of two ladders, one with its foot at (0, 0) and the other with its foot at (10, 0).

Find the coordinates where they cross.

Find some pairs of ladders that cross at *integer* coordinates.

Now start by choosing a *point* and try to find ladders that cross there.

How many pairs of ladders can you find that cross at (3, 4), for example?

Can you find a connection between the equations of a pair of ladders and the place where they cross?

18

Make Twenty-Four

Introduction

This lesson exploits the classic puzzle in which you are asked to make the number 24 using four given starting numbers and standard mathematical operations. There are many related problems, such as the 'four fours' problem – trying to make as many numbers as possible just using common mathematical symbols and (exactly or up to, depending on the rules) four number 4s. See: http://paulbourke.net/fun/4444/

Depending on your purposes, you might decide not to allow calculators, so that learners are practising their arithmetic, or to allow them so that they can focus more on their strategies and considering all possible options.

Aims and outcomes

- Practise integer mental arithmetic on +, –, × and ÷ calculations.
- Understand conventions relating to the priority of operations.

Lesson starter (10 minutes)

Suppose you have the numbers 1, 2, 3 and 4 and you have to use each number exactly once. *You can combine them using +, –, × and ÷ (and brackets), with as many or as few operations as you like. See how many positive integers you can make in 3 minutes.*

For example, all the integers from 1 to 24 are possible: one example for each is given in the table below, but clearly there are more.

1	$(4 - 3) \times (2 - 1)$		12	$2 \times (4 - 1 + 3)$
2	$1 + 2 + 3 - 4$		13	$3 \times (1 + 2) + 4$
3	$\dfrac{2 + 4}{3 - 1}$		14	$1 \times 2 \times (3 + 4)$
			15	$3 \times (4 - 1 + 2)$
4	$4 - 1 - 2 + 3$		16	$2 \times (1 + 3 + 4)$
5	$(1 + 4) \times (3 - 2)$		17	$3 \times (1 + 4) + 2$
6	$1 - 2 + 3 + 4$		18	$1 \times 3 \times (2 + 4)$
7	$3 \times (2 - 1) + 4$		19	$3 \times (2 + 4) + 1$
8	$4 - 1 + 2 + 3$		20	$1 \times (2 + 3) \times 4$
9	$2 \times 3 + 4 - 1$		21	$3 \times (1 + 2 + 4)$
10	$1 + 2 + 3 + 4$		22	$2 \times (3 \times 4 - 1)$
11	$2 \times 3 + 4 + 1$		23	$2 \times 3 \times 4 - 1$

24	$1 \times 2 \times 3 \times 4$

Main lesson (30 minutes)

Now we're going to fix the target number. We saw that we could make 24 by doing $1 \times 2 \times 3 \times 4$. Which other sets of four numbers allow us to make 24?

Give out the Task Sheets and encourage learners to try the various problems. You may wish to encourage learners to try to write their computations in one line, using brackets if necessary, rather than as separate multi-steps:

For example: $4 \times (5 + 7 - 6)$ rather than
$$5 + 7 = 12$$
$$12 - 6 = 6$$
$$4 \times 6 = 24$$

It is easy to do this in this context, since when a learner writes '12' at the end of the first line, for instance, you can say: 'You're not allowed to write '12'!', since it isn't 4, 5, 6 or 7. It would certainly be worth discouraging *Countdown*-style 'linked equals signs' such as:

$$5 + 7 = 12 - 6 = 6 \times 4 = 24$$

where the equals signs relate only to the first term following them, not to the whole expression!

Plenary (15 minutes)

What did you find out? Which ones could you do? Were there any you thought couldn't *be done? Which? Why?*

One solution for each is given in the following table.

Set of four positive integers	One way of making 24
2, 3, 4, 5	$2 \times (3 + 4 + 5)$
3, 4, 5, 6	$6 \times (3 + 5 - 4)$
4, 5, 6, 7	$4 \times (5 + 7 - 6)$
5, 6, 7, 8	$6 \times (7 - 8 + 5)$
6, 7, 8, 9	$\dfrac{6 \times 8}{9 - 7}$
7, 8, 9, 10	$\dfrac{8 \times 9}{10 - 7}$
8, 9, 10, 11	impossible

Solutions from http://home.manhattan.edu/~peter.boothe/24solutions/, with kind permission from Peter Boothe.

Particularly difficult sets of numbers, because the solutions involve fractions, are: 1, 3, 4, 6 and 1, 4, 5, 6. Solutions for these are $\dfrac{6}{1 - \frac{3}{4}}$ and $\dfrac{6}{\frac{5}{4} - 1}$.

Homework (5 minutes)

Can you make 24 using four of the same *number, e.g. 1, 1, 1 and 1? Why / why not?*

From (1, 1, 1, 1) to (24, 24, 24, 24), the following are the only ones that can be done (although they may be possible in more than one way):

$$3 \times 3 \times 3 - 3 = 24 \qquad\qquad 12 + 12 + 12 - 12 = 24$$

$$4 \times 4 + 4 + 4 = 24 \qquad\qquad \frac{22 + 22}{22} + 22 = 24$$

$$5 \times 5 - \frac{5}{5} = 24 \qquad\qquad \frac{23 \times 23 + 23}{23} = 24$$

$$6 + 6 + 6 + 6 = 24 \qquad\qquad (24 - 24) \times 24 + 24 = 24$$

To make it harder

Learners who find this relatively straightforward could consider the following questions.

Are some target numbers easier to make, with a certain set of four integers, than others? Why / why not? Try to find an impossible *target number. Can you be sure that it definitely cannot be made?*

More information is available at: http://home.manhattan.edu/~peter.boothe/24solutions/

To make it easier

Learners who find this hard could begin by exploring what numbers they can make with the four given numbers, without worrying too much initially about getting to 24. Ideas may come as they produce more numbers; for example, getting '12' and seeing how to find a '2' to do '2' × '12'.

Make Twenty-Four

The target number is 24.

You can use as many of the operations +, −, × and ÷ (and brackets) as you like.

You must use each number exactly once.

Can you make 24 using these sets of numbers?

2,	3,	4,	5
3,	4,	5,	6
4,	5,	6,	7
5,	6,	7,	8
6,	7,	8,	9
7,	8,	9,	10
8,	9,	10,	11

What other sets of four positive integers can you use to make 24?

Which do you think are harder and which do you think are easier? Why?

19

Meeting Up

Introduction

One of the affordances of graph-drawing software is the way in which a wrong graph can be instantly removed without any rubbing out. This 'no mess' aspect encourages a trial and improvement mentality in which learners can develop their previous attempts, in this lesson getting closer to the desired lines. Numerical estimation is also helpful, when learners judge by eye how near to other lines the new line needs to be.

Aims and outcomes

- Understand how the equation of a straight-line graph controls its gradient and y-intercept.
- Use coordinates to find positions in two dimensions.

Lesson starter (10 minutes)

Project or draw this image:

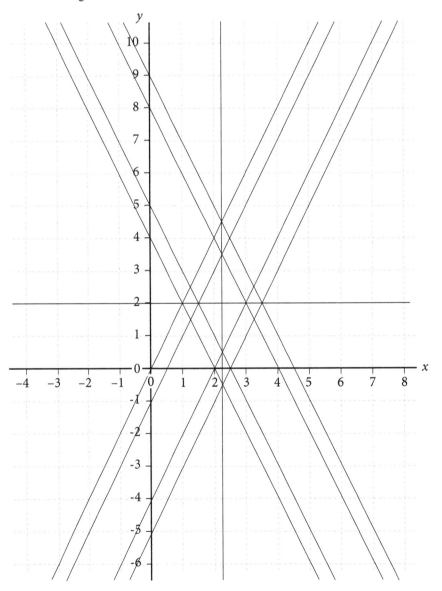

What are the equations of the lines?

Learners can choose a line and examine the coordinates of points that lie along it, looking for connections. Or they can consider the gradient and the *y*-intercept.

The 10 lines are:

$y = 2x$	$y = -2x + 9$
$y = 2x - 1$	$y = -2x + 8$
$y = 2x - 4$	$y = -2x + 5$
$y = 2x - 5$	$y = -2x + 4$
$x = 2.25$	$y = 2$

These may be quite difficult to find, and some trial and error may be necessary. Ideally, you will be able to use graph-drawing software to enter the equations suggested by learners, to see how close they come to the picture. This models to learners how they can experiment with the software themselves in the main lesson.

Main lesson (30 minutes)

Give out the Task Sheets and encourage lots of experimenting and recording of equations.

Plenary (15 minutes)

Did you manage to make all the 12 lines? Did you make your own pattern of lines? What did you find out?

The equations of the 12 lines are:

$y = \frac{1}{2}x + 2$	$y = -\frac{1}{2}x + 4$
$y = x + 1$	$y = -x + 5$
$y = 2x - 1$	$y = -2x + 7$
$y = 3x - 3$	$y = -3x + 9$
$y = 4x - 5$	$y = -4x + 11$
$x = 2$	$y = 3$

In general, lines passing through (a, b) will have equations $y = m(x - a) + b$, where m is a constant, along with the vertical line $x = a$. So, apart from $x = a$, all the graphs will have equations $y = mx + (b - ma)$. For example, graphs passing through $(1, 2)$ will have the form $y = mx - m + 2$.

Homework (5 minutes)

Summarize the effect of the equation of a graph on how it looks. Draw three examples to illustrate your statements.

To make it harder

Learners comfortable with this task could design straight-line graph patterns, print them out, swap them with each other, and then attempt to reproduce them by discovering the correct equations.

To make it easier

Learners who find this hard could begin by being asked to find, by experimentation, a graph that passes through $(2, 3)$, and then another, and another.

What is the same and what is different about the graphs?

Alternatively, learners could begin by exploring graphs of the form $y = mx$, that pass through the origin.

Meeting Up

The 12 lines below all pass through the point (2, 3).

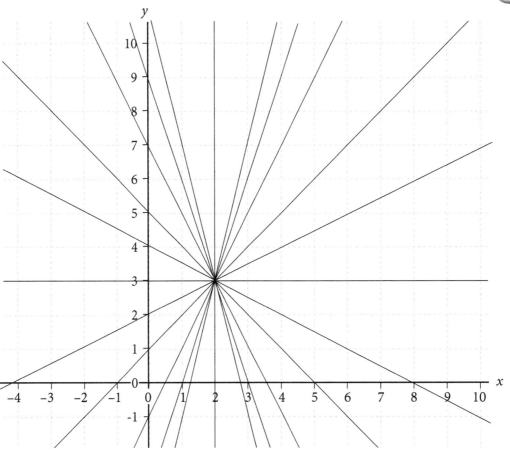

Using graph-drawing software, enter equations that will produce these 12 lines.

Now choose a different point.

Make up another 12 equations that all go through your chosen point.

What patterns are there in the equations of lines that all go through the same point?

Can you explain the patterns?

Can you invent a rule for writing down a list of equations that all go through a particular point?

20 Mystery Messages

Introduction

Learners can get very excited about code-breaking tasks. This lesson introduces the method of *frequency analysis* as a way of cracking a substitution code. Different letters of the alphabet occur with different relative frequencies, and these are reasonably constant from one piece of writing to another. It is possible to exploit this by finding out which letters in the coded message occur most often, as these are most likely to be E, T, A, etc. – the letters which come up most frequently in the English language.

Aims and outcomes

- Construct a frequency table from given data.
- Represent data graphically.
- Use statistical analysis to break a code.

Lesson starter (15 minutes)

What is unusual about this piece of prose? (You could display it via a data projector or – harder for the learners – read it aloud.)

> Branton Hills was a small town in a rich agricultural district; and having many a possibility for growth. But, through a sort of smug satisfaction with conditions of long ago, had no thought of improving such important adjuncts as roads; putting up public buildings, nor laying out parks; in fact a dormant, slowly dying community. So satisfactory was its status that it had no form of transportation to surrounding towns but by railroad, or 'old Dobbin'. Now, any town thus isolating its inhabitants, will invariably find this big, busy world passing it by; glancing at it, curiously, as at an odd animal at a circus; and, you will find, caring not a whit about its condition. Naturally, a town should grow. You can look upon it as a child; which, through natural conditions, should attain manhood; and add to its surrounding thriving districts its products of farm, shop, or factory. It should show a spirit of association with surrounding towns; crawl out of its lair, and find how backward it is.

> Ernest Vincent Wright, *Gadsby: Champion of Youth* (1939)

If learners need a clue say: '*It's eeeeasy!*' or ask: '*What's missing?*'

It is a *lipogram*, which does not include the letter E. The entire book (over 50 000 words), from which this is taken, contains not a single letter E! Learners might like to try writing a short paragraph without using the letter E.

Main lesson (25 minutes)

Give out the Task Sheets and encourage learners to think about what the graph could represent. It shows the average frequencies of the letters of the alphabet in English text. Alternatively, you could dispense with the Task Sheet and ask learners to construct such a table by counting the letters in a page of a book or newspaper. A faster way, if you have access to computers, is to paste a large amount of text into a word-processing package and then use the 'find and replace' feature to replace all 'a's or 'A's with 'α', all 'b's or 'B's with 'β', etc. Each time, the software will tell you how many replacements it has made, and you can record these numbers in a spreadsheet.

Plenary (15 minutes)

Frequency analysis of the coded message (137 letters) gives the following table and graph:

Letter	Number of occurrences	Relative frequency (correct to 2 decimal places)
A	0	0.00
B	1	0.01
C	0	0.00
D	4	0.03
E	0	0.00
F	8	0.06
G	5	0.04
H	6	0.04
I	3	0.02
J	20	0.15
K	4	0.03
L	2	0.01
M	5	0.04
N	9	0.07
O	1	0.01
P	1	0.01
Q	5	0.04
R	3	0.02
S	9	0.07
T	7	0.05
U	1	0.01
V	1	0.01
W	7	0.05
X	12	0.09
Y	14	0.10
Z	9	0.07

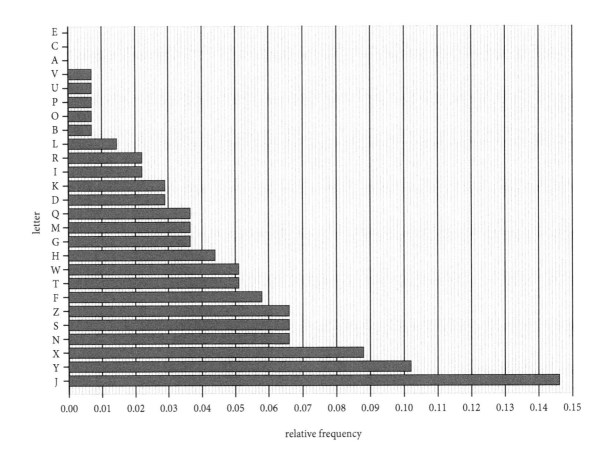

The much higher frequency for 'J' strongly suggests that it is E and that 'Y' is T, in both cases a five-steps-forward shift. Moving *all* letters five steps backwards in the alphabet gives the message:

> JULIUS CAESAR USED SUBSTITUTION CODES TO COMMUNICATE WITH HIS GENERALS. THEY ARE SIMPLE TO USE BUT CAN BE BROKEN BY ANALYSING THE FREQUENCY OF THE DIFFERENT LETTERS.

 The following website can be useful for decoding messages like the one above: www.secretcode-breaker.com/caesar-cipher.html

Homework (5 minutes)

Learners could find out about *public-key cryptography* and how it works. They could also explore the relative frequencies of letters of the alphabet in other languages.

To make it harder

Learners who quickly crack the code could consider the following:

What happens if you write a lipogram *and then code it. Would it be easy to spot? Would it be very hard to decode? Try it.*

To make it easier

Learners who find this hard could begin by making up a sentence and then writing each letter of it on a separate piece of card. Place all the cards in a dark plastic bag and choose one at random. Which letter do they think they are most likely to pull out? It won't necessarily be an 'E'. It depends on the sentence that they choose.

Mystery Messages

What do you think this graph is showing?

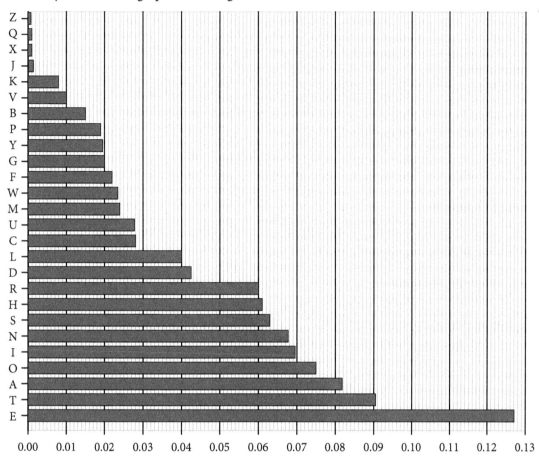

What labels would you put on the axes?

What labels would you put on the axes?

Can you work out what this says?

OZQNZX HFJXFW ZXJI XZGXYNYZYNTS HTIJX YT HTRRZSNHFYJ BNYM MNX
LJSJWFQX. YMJD FWJ XNRUQJ YT ZXJ GZY HFS GJ GWTPJS GD FSFQDXNS
L YMJ KWJVZJSHD TK YMJ INKKJWJSY QJYYJWX.

Explain how you did it.

Make up a mystery message for someone else to work out.

21

Newspaper Pages

Introduction

Books are obviously familiar objects, especially in school, but have learners ever thought much about how they are produced? This lesson gives learners an opportunity to think about how the pages are numbered on the sheets that go to make up a book. Beginning with newspapers, some simple connections allow learners to predict which pages will come on the same sheets of paper as each other. The topic of pagination can lead to some interesting mathematics.

Aims and outcomes

- Find a connection between an increasing and a decreasing sequence.
- Use linear integer sequences to solve problems.

Lesson starter (10 minutes)

If you tear out a page from your exercise book, what happens? Why?

Lots of things – you get into trouble, perhaps, but also a page falls out at the back.

Which page? Why?

Learners may have a sense that if you go in four pages at the front, say, the loose page will be the one four pages from the back.

We're going to think about the page numbers in newspapers. How many sheets of paper do you think you need to make a 20-page newspaper? Why?

Each sheet of newspaper has four pages on it, so you need only five sheets of paper.

Which page numbers are on the third *sheet of paper? Why?*

This may tax learners' imaginations. The answer is (5, 6; 15, 16). They may think that 'add 1, add 10, add 11' is the rule, and although this is wrong you could leave this hanging for the next part of the lesson.

Main lesson (30 minutes)

Bring in just one page from a newspaper and hold it up or pass it round.

What can you say about the newspaper this came from?

(Or take one page out of each of several newspapers in the staffroom – use yesterday's papers unless you want to be very unpopular! – so that each group can have one page from a different newspaper, and therefore a slightly different problem to work on.)

Learners may comment on the title of the paper and other content-related factors.

How many pages do you think the original paper had? Why?

Give out the Task Sheets and encourage learners to think about the problem. You could provide other (complete) newspapers or they could use scrap paper to mock up their own.

Plenary (15 minutes)

What do you think the other page numbers are? Why? What connections did you find?

There are 120 pages in the newspaper. For an n-page newspaper, the rth sheet will contain the pages $(2r - 1, 2r; n - 2r + 1, n - 2r + 2)$. The total of these comes to $2n + 2$, since the r's cancel out. So the total of the four page numbers on any sheet will always be twice the total number of pages in the paper plus 2. So given the four numbers it is fairly easy to find the total number of pages in the paper. However, making up correct puzzles, in which the four numbers given are a possible set of four numbers is harder.

Learners may invent puzzles like this, which are not correct: 'A page taken from a newspaper has page numbers 11, 25, 45, 51. How many pages are there in the entire paper?' This gives $n = 66$, but in fact those four page numbers clearly cannot be on the same sheet. Learners might even construct puzzles involving four *even* page numbers, which is clearly impossible. That the total of the four numbers is an even number is a necessary but not a sufficient condition. But any pair of consecutive (odd, even) numbers will work.

Homework (5 minutes)

Look at one page in a newspaper and come up with as many mathematical questions as you can about it – these could relate to the content as well as the page numbers. If possible, bring in the page, as well as your questions. (Remember to ask permission if it isn't your paper!)

To make it harder

Confident learners could consider how a newspaper might be made from one or more large sheets of paper, which are folded several times and then cut. *Which way round do the pages need to be placed? Why?*

To make it easier

Starting with two sheets of scrap paper and making an eight-page newspaper may be a good way to begin if learners find this difficult.

Newspaper Pages

One sheet is removed from a newspaper. The page numbers on it are 37, 38, 83 and 84.

What can you tell about the original newspaper? Why?

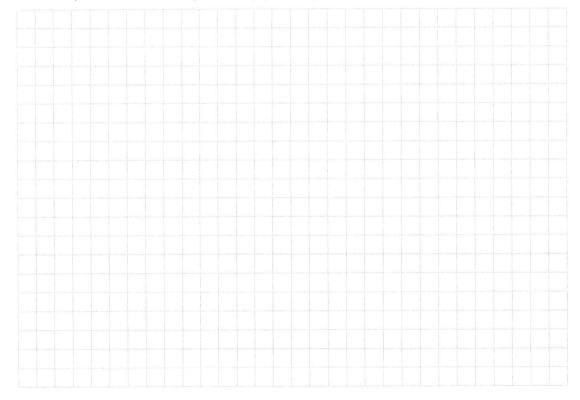

Make up some problems like this.

Explain how to make up problems like this.

22

One Cut

Introduction

This lesson consists of a very open task in which learners are asked to find all possible shapes that can be made by folding once and cutting (along a straight line) a square piece of paper. This can provoke much thinking about geometrical properties. You could amaze learners with the famous 'squircle' magic trick (search for 'around the square' on www.youtube.com for a short film of it) at some point in this lesson, but do make sure that you check all the way through any clips beforehand to ensure suitability.

Aims and outcomes

- Understand and use the properties of different polygons.
- Use symmetry to solve geometrical problems.

Lesson starter (10 minutes)

Hold up a postcard (or similarly sized piece of card).

Do you think I could cut a hole in this postcard big enough for me to walk through?

Maybe someone will have seen the trick before, in which case perhaps they could demonstrate it. If anyone says yes, ask them to do it. (It would be helpful to have several postcards available as spares.)

Fold the postcard in half:

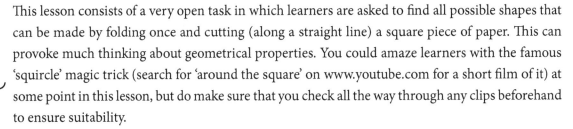

Cut along the dotted lines marked below. The more lines you make, the bigger the hole will be when you open it out.

Also cut along the fold line, *but not all the way*, just through the portion shown in bold below:

Don't cut through all the way to the outer edges!

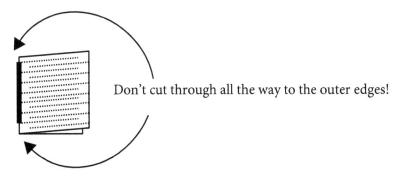

Open it out and, if you have made enough slices, you will have a loop large enough to climb through.

How does it work?

There are links here to maximizing the perimeter for a fixed area.

Main lesson (30 minutes)

Give out the Task Sheets and encourage learners to follow the instructions carefully. There are many possible shapes to find.

Plenary (15 minutes)

What shapes did you get? How did you get them?

Even with a simple folding of the square in half, along a fold line parallel to a pair of opposite edges, considering all possible different cuts leads to the following possible shapes.

a. Two rectangles (congruent or not).

b. Three rectangles (at least two congruent).

c. Two congruent right-angled triangles and a convex hexagon with two right angles and one line of symmetry.

d. Two congruent right-angled triangles and a convex pentagon with two right angles and one line of symmetry.

e. Two congruent right-angled triangles and an isosceles triangle.

f. An isosceles triangle and a concave pentagon with two right angles and a line of symmetry.

g. An isosceles triangle and a concave heptagon with four right angles and a line of symmetry.

h. An isosceles triangle and two congruent right-angled trapeziums.

More complicated folds will lead to even more possible shapes. For more information about this, see Demaine, E. D. and Lubiw, A. (2004) 'Folding and Cutting Paper', *Discrete and Computational Geometry, Lecture Notes in Computer Science*, 1763, 104–18.

Homework (5 minutes)

There are many sets of instructions on the internet telling you how to make a five-pointed star using flat folds and just one straight cut. Find out how to do it and be ready to show us next lesson. Or invent your own way of making an impressive-looking shape.

To make it harder

Confident learners could try to work out a folding pattern that, with one straight cut, will generate a particular shape of their choice. For more information, see http://erikdemaine.org/foldcut/ and http://citeseerx.ist.psu.edu/viewdoc/download?doi=10.1.1.119.3302&rep=rep1&type=pdf

To make it easier

An easier way to begin would be to make one straight cut without folding the paper at all.

How many possible different shapes can you make doing this?

One Cut

Take a square piece of paper and make a flat fold anyhow you like.

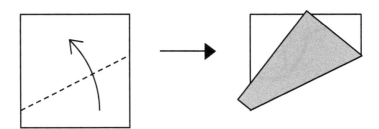

Make one straight cut in any direction you choose, but it must go from one edge of the paper all the way to the other.

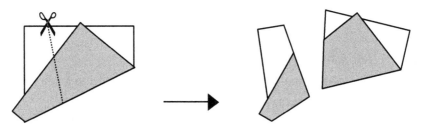

Then open the pieces and describe what shapes you have got.

© Colin Foster (2011) *Resources for Teaching Mathematics 11–14*. London: Continuum

What possible shapes do you think you can make in this way?

Are there any shapes that you *don't* think you can make? Why?

What if you folded more than once before the cut?
The cut must still be *one straight cut*.

23

Palindromic Numbers

Introduction

This lesson uses a cross-curricular idea from English and applies it to numbers, leading to many possible puzzles. Palindromes are words (such as DAD) which read the same forwards and backwards. If the date happens to be palindromic when written in some particular format (e.g. 3/1/13 or 4/10/2014), that might make a good day to do this work. Otherwise, learners could work out how long it is until the next palindromic date.

Aims and outcomes

- Practise calculations leading to palindromic numbers.
- Investigate an iterating process leading to palindromic numbers.

Lesson starter (15 minutes)

Look at these sentences:

Never odd or even.	I prefer pi!
Marge lets Norah see Sharon's telegram.	Did Hannah see bees? Hannah did!
Was it a car or a cat I saw?	Won't I panic in a pit now?
Rise to vote, Sir!	Mr Owl ate my metal worm.

What do all these sentences have in common? Can you make up some more like them?

(If you happen to have someone in the class with a palindromic name, such as Anna or Eve, you could point to them as a clue.) All these sentences are palindromic: ignoring the spaces and punctuation, and reading the letters in reverse order, makes exactly the same sentence. A single word, like MUM, which does this is called a palindrome.

Find palindromes (single words) with different numbers of letters. Can you find an n-letter palindrome where n = 1, 2, 3, 4, . . ., 10?

n	Examples of *n*-letter palindromes
1	a, I (any one-letter word)
2	ee, oo
3	pop, eye
4	toot, deed
5	madam, level, kayak, radar, rotor, civic, stats
6	Hannah, redder
7	racecar (a Toyota?), rotator, re-paper
8	Idappadi (a city in Tamil Nadu, India)
9	rotavator, Malayalam (a language in southern India)
10	Zirak Kariz (a region in Afghanistan)
11	de-tartrated (a term from chemistry meaning to remove a tartrate)

Main lesson (25 minutes)

How many three-digit palindromic numbers are there? How many four-digit?

There are 90 of each – the same amount, which may surprise learners! This is bound to happen, since the two middle digits in a four-digit palindrome have to be the same, just as the first and last digits do. For a three-digit number, there are nine choices for the first digit and then ten choices for the middle digit – and the third digit has to be the same as the first, so $9 \times 10 = 90$. One-digit numbers are considered (trivially) to be palindromic. And of course there are nine two-digit palindromic numbers (11, 22, 33, 44, 55, 66, 77, 88 and 99). Learners could explore this pattern further.

Give out the Task Sheets and encourage learners to follow the flow diagram carefully and investigate different numbers.

Plenary (15 minutes)

What did you find out? Which numbers did you try?

What was the greatest number of steps any of your numbers needed? What was the smallest?

The results for the numbers 1 to 100 are shown in the table. Doing this is less work than you might think, since each number must work the same as its reverse. The main problem is the hugely greater number of steps needed for 89 (or 98).

n	No. of steps	Palindrome	*n*	No. of steps	Palindrome	*n*	No. of steps	Palindrome
1	0	1	21	1	33	41	1	55
2	0	2	22	0	22	42	1	66
3	0	3	23	1	55	43	1	77
4	0	4	24	1	66	44	0	44
5	0	5	25	1	77	45	1	99
6	0	6	26	1	88	46	2	121
7	0	7	27	1	99	47	1	121
8	0	8	28	2	121	48	2	363
9	0	9	29	1	121	49	2	484
10	**1**	**11**	30	1	33	50	1	55
11	0	11	31	1	44	51	1	66
12	1	33	32	1	55	52	1	77
13	1	44	33	0	33	53	1	88
14	1	55	34	1	77	54	1	99
15	1	66	35	1	88	55	0	55
16	1	77	36	1	99	56	1	121
17	1	88	37	2	121	57	2	363
18	1	99	38	1	121	58	2	484
19	**2**	**121**	39	2	363	**59**	**3**	**1111**
20	1	22	40	1	44	60	1	66

Resources for Teaching Mathematics 11–14
TEACHER SHEET

n	No. of steps	Palindrome	n	No. of steps	Palindrome
61	1	77	81	1	99
62	1	88	82	2	121
63	1	99	83	1	121
64	2	121	84	2	363
65	1	121	85	2	484
66	0	66	86	3	1111
67	2	484	87	4	4884
68	3	1111	88	0	88
69	**4**	**4884**	**89**	**24**	**8 813 200 023 188**
70	1	77	90	1	99
71	1	88	91	2	121
72	1	99	92	1	121
73	2	121	93	2	363
74	1	121	94	2	484
75	2	363	95	3	1111
76	2	484	96	4	4884
77	0	77	97	6	44 044
78	4	4884	98	24	8 813 200 023 188
79	**6**	**44 044**	99	**0**	**99**
80	1	88	100	1	101

No one knows whether *all* numbers eventually get to palindromes. The number 196 has been tried for millions of stages but does not seem to yield a palindrome. Such numbers are called *Lychrel numbers*. See www.jasondoucette.com/196.html for more information.

Homework (5 minutes)

Learners could be asked to find some palindromic *squares* (such as 1, 4, 9, 121, 484, 676, 10 201, 12 321, 14 641, 40 804, 44 944, . . .) or palindromic *primes*, for instance (such as 2, 3, 5, 7, 11, 101, 131, 151, 181, 191, . . .). What about other special palindromic numbers?

To make it harder

Keen learners could investigate which palindromic numbers are divisible by 11. The answer is every one which contains an even number of digits.

To make it easier

Once they understand the process, all learners should be able to try putting some numbers through the flow diagram, perhaps using a calculator to aid the arithmetic and allow them to focus on what is happening.

Palindromic Numbers

Try putting numbers into this flow diagram.

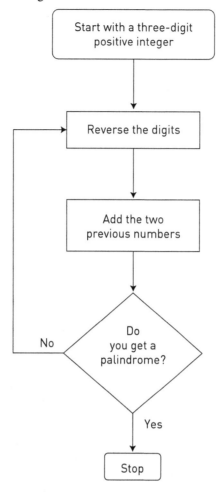

For example, starting with 358 you get:

$$358 + 853 = 1211$$
$$1211 + 1121 = 2332$$

which is a palindrome in 2 steps.

What happens with different starting numbers?

What if they don't have three digits?

Do you think that all starting numbers eventually get to a palindrome?

How many steps do different numbers take?

24

Percentage Puzzles

Introduction

Percentages are ubiquitous in everyday life, so it is clearly important that learners develop sufficient fluency with them to feel at home using and interpreting percentage statements. This lesson takes a mental non-calculator approach, and lots of practice should be necessary to solve the puzzle. Some careful thinking will be needed if learners are to construct good puzzles of a similar kind.

Aims and outcomes

- Calculate percentages of a given quantity.
- Interpret percentage statements accurately.

Lesson starter (10 minutes)

No calculators, please, for today's lesson.

Which do you think is bigger: 40% of £60 or 60% of £40? Why?

Students may argue that 60% is more than half, whereas 40% is less than half, so 60% must be more, but they are percentages of different things. On the other hand, they may think that a slice of £60 sounds like more than a slice of £40, even if the slices are not the same proportion. However, they are exactly equal.

Does this always work? Can you make up other examples?

Yes, *a*% of *b* is always the same as *b*% of *a*, because $\frac{a}{100} \times b = \frac{b}{100} \times a$. This follows from the commutativity of multiplication.

Can you think of situations when knowing this might be useful – say, if you were calculating percentages mentally?

It can be handy when doing a 'hard' percentage of an 'easy' amount – you can exchange it for an 'easy' percentage of a 'harder' amount. For example, 36% of £50 may sound difficult, but 50% of £36 is just half of £36, which is £18, so that's the answer to 36% of £50 too.

Main lesson (30 minutes)

Give out the Task Sheets. The puzzle may be more difficult than learners expect, since you can make some correct statements at the start but then the remaining numbers will not fit in the gaps that are left. The idea is that learners will need to do some trial and improvement and repeatedly calculate percentages mentally to see get the numbers to fit.

Plenary (15 minutes)

Did you manage to place all the 15 numbers correctly? Was it easy? Why/why not?

Were some numbers easier to deal with than others? Why?/why not?

Did you have to go back and move numbers later? Which ones?

Since the five lines are identical, the answers can, of course, be listed in any order. Also, because of the equality discussed in the starter, *a*% of *b* can always be written the other way round as *b*% of *a*.

The answers are:

2% of 50 = 1	or	50% of 2 = 1
10% of 60 = 6	or	60% of 10 = 6
15% of 20 = 3	or	20% of 15 = 3
25% of 100 = 25	or	100% of 25 = 25
40% of 50 = 20	or	50% of 40 = 20

Homework (5 minutes)

Here is another percentages puzzle. Percentages go down the side and amounts along the top. Each cell in the table gives the answer.

Can you see why this must be 80? Can you complete the table?

Percentage	Amount				
		20			**40**
			45	225	
		1			
					12
10%	8				
			36		24

This is more like a traditional tables square. The answers are:

	80	20	60	300	40
75%	60	15	45	225	30
5%	4	1	3	15	2
30%	24	6	18	90	12
10%	8	2	6	30	4
60%	48	12	36	180	24

To make it harder

There should be plenty of scope for learners to make this more challenging by their choice of numbers or by increasing from five rows of statements to more than five rows. Aiming for a unique solution is also difficult.

To make it easier

Learners who struggle with the initial puzzle could begin by writing three percentage statements, using 9 different numbers, and then create a puzzle from this for someone else to do. Doing this may make the process of solving the given puzzle easier.

Percentage Puzzles

Place these 15 numbers, once each, into the 15 spaces below so that the calculations are correct.

$$1, 2, 3, 6, 10, 15, 20, 20, 25, 25, 40, 50, 50, 60, 100$$

_____ % of _____ = _____

_____ % of _____ = _____

_____ % of _____ = _____

_____ % of _____ = _____

_____ % of _____ = _____

© Colin Foster (2011) *Resources for Teaching Mathematics 11–14*. London: Continuum

Do you think it can be done in more than one way? Why/why not?

Make up a percentages puzzle like this for someone else to solve.

Can you make an easier version and a harder version?

25

Pizza Slices

Introduction

Slices of pizza are a staple of mathematics textbooks – where would the teaching of fractions be without them? Sometimes pseudo-real-life mathematics problems involve cutting pizzas into implausible numbers of slices, such as 11. In this lesson, Learners consider the way pizza companies actually do cut up their pizzas and use their knowledge of sectors to work out how the areas of the slices taken from different-sized pizzas compare.

Aims and outcomes

- Calculate the area of a sector of a circle.
- Consider linear and area scale factors.

Lesson starter (10 minutes)

Work out the volume of a pizza that is a cylinder of radius z and thickness a.

This will be the circular area multiplied by the thickness. This leads to the formula $\pi z^2 a$, which, putting 'pi' for π, could be written as '*pizza*'!

Can you make up some more formulae like this?

Learners might find a GCSE formula sheet useful for ideas.

This is hard and answers are going to be contrived but still fun. A biscuit with dimensions b, i and c would have volume '*bic*'. The surface area of a cylinder of diameter p and length e is πpe, or '*pipe*'. A trapezium with parallel sides of lengths a and p separated by a distance y has an area formula '*happy*', where the 'h' stands for 'half' and one of the ps stands for 'plus' ('half a plus p, times y'), but by this stage we are getting quite silly!

Keen learners could find out about *Tupper's self-referential formula*.

Main lesson (30 minutes)

Give out the Task Sheets. *Look at the data at the top about the four different sizes of pizza. What things do you notice?*

Learners may make all kinds of comments, but are likely to mention that as the pizzas get bigger they are cut into more slices. But to what extent do these two factors cancel each other out?

Suppose we buy one each of these four sizes of pizza. How many slices would that be altogether?

This comes to $6 + 8 + 10 + 12 = 36$, which should be enough for a slice each for everyone in the class. (Learners could calculate this by doing 9×4, taking 9 as the average, or some other shortcut method.)

If I laid out the four pizzas here, all sliced into pieces and said you could go first, and you wanted the biggest slice, which pizza would you take a slice from? Why?

Some learners may think that they are all equal in size; others may think it would be better to take a slice of the biggest pizza, since it is the biggest; others may think that it would be better to take from the smallest pizza, since it is split into the fewest pieces; others may compromise and go for a medium or XL pizza. This should generate some disagreement, which could lead in to the rest of the work on the Task Sheet.

Plenary (15 minutes)

What results did you get? Which pizza has the biggest pieces? Why do you think that this happens?

	S	M	XL	XXL
Diameter (inches)	9.5	11.5	13.5	15.5
Number of slices	6	8	10	12
Area of one slice (square inches)	11.81	12.98	14.31	15.72
Length of crust on one slice (inches)	4.97	4.52	4.24	4.06
Perimeter of one slice (inches)	14.47	16.02	17.74	19.56

The number of slices is increasing *arithmetically*, but this cannot keep pace with the *quadratic* increase in the area of the pizzas, so the area of a slice of pizza does get bigger as the pizza diameter increases. So does the perimeter of a slice, but the amount of crust decreases.

If we keep the four diameters the same as they are given and stick with 6 slices for the small pizza, we can keep the amounts of pizza in one slice more similar for the larger pizzas by dividing them into more pieces. We have an arithmetic sequence of diameters and thus a quadratic sequence of areas, but only an arithmetic sequences in the number of pieces, leading to an increasing disparity as the pizzas get larger. Let the nth pizza in the sequence have diameter $(7.5 + 2n)$ inches. Then its area will be $\frac{\pi(7.5 + 2n)^2}{4}$ and, if it is split into k equal sectors, each will have area $\frac{\pi(7.5 + 2n)^2}{4k}$.

To keep this quantity as near to constant as possible, as n changes, $k_1 : k_2 : k_3 : k_4 = (7.5 + 2)^2 : (7.5 + 4)^2 : (7.5 + 6)^2 : (7.5 + 8)^2 = 9.5^2 : 11.5^2 : 13.5^2 : 15.5^2$, since $k \propto d^2$, where d is the diameter. This gives the ratio $90.25 : 132.25 : 182.25 : 240.25 = 361 : 529 : 729 : 961 \approx 2 : 3 : 4 : 5$, leading, perhaps, to a suggestion of 6, 9, 12 and 16 slices. This choice would produce the data in the table below, where now it is the extra-large pizza that has the largest slices.

	S	M	XL	XXL
Diameter (inches)	9.5	11.5	13.5	15.5
Number of slices	6	9	12	16
Area of one slice (square inches)	11.81	11.54	11.93	11.79
Length of crust on one slice (inches)	4.97	4.01	3.53	3.04
Perimeter of one slice (inches)	14.47	15.51	17.03	18.54

Homework (5 minutes)

Learners could examine the number of slices in different-sized pizzas offered by local pizza companies. Do any of them vary their numbers of slices in a different way? Is it better for bigger pizzas to have larger slices or do they become too narrow and hard to hold (floppy)?

To make it harder

Learners confident with this work could consider how the patterns would continue with larger and larger diameters of pizza. This is a race between a quadratic sequence (areas) and arithmetic sequence (number of slices), in which the quadratic will win.

To make it easier

Learners who find this very hard could begin with a 6-inch pizza divided into 6 pieces and compare this with a 7-inch pizza divided into 7 pieces, an 8-inch pizza divided into 8 pieces, etc. In general, one slice of an n-inch pizza, divided into n slices, will have an area of $\frac{\pi n^2}{4n} = \frac{\pi n}{4}$, so the area is proportional to n. So by the time we reach a 12-inch pizza, each $\frac{1}{12}$ slice is twice as big as the $\frac{1}{6}$ slices of the 6-inch pizza were.

Pizza Slices

Here are some data about four different sizes of pizza: small (S), medium (M), extra large (XL) and extra extra large (XXL).

9.5″	11.5″	13.5″	15.5″
6 slices	8 slices	10 slices	12 slices
S	**M**	**XL**	**XXL**

Work out the *area of one slice* of each different size of pizza.

Work out the *length of crust* of each different slice.

Work out the *perimeter* of each different slice.

What patterns do you find? Can you explain them?

Suppose you want one slice of *any* pizza to be about the same size. Can you choose better values for the number of slices there should be in each size of pizza?

26

Rectilinear Shapes

Introduction

Rectilinear shapes (polygons containing only 90° and 270° angles) crop up quite a bit in 'real life'; to a good approximation, the rooms in many modern buildings have a rectilinear shape when viewed from above. There are some interesting facts concerning the edges and the angles, which learners will investigate in this lesson, drawing on their knowledge of angles in polygons more generally.

Aims and outcomes

- Explore patterns in a family of polygons.
- Use exterior angles in polygons to solve problems.

Lesson starter (15 minutes)

A robot can move one unit right (R), left (L), up (U) or down (D) in two dimensions. Try to imagine the movement described by:

    R R U R R D L L D R L L U

What can you say about this movement?
> *Does the robot get back to where it started? Why/why not?*
> Yes, it does.
> *Does it ever cross its own path? Why/why not?*
> *Try to develop some way of answering this without drawing or imagining the whole journey.*
> *Make up another journey that gets the robot back to where it started.*

An R and an L cancel each other out, as do a U and a D. So using $n(R)$ to represent the total number of letter Rs in the journey, etc., if $n(R) = n(L)$ and $n(U) = n(D)$, then the robot has returned to its starting position. If not, then its final position is $n(R) - n(L)$ places to the right and $n(U) - n(D)$ places up from where it began.

Main lesson (25 minutes)

Give out the Task Sheets. Squared paper would be useful. Some learners may benefit from being encouraged to draw simpler shapes to begin with. However, provided they are careful they should get equally useful data from more complex rectilinear shapes.

Plenary (15 minutes)

What did you discover? Were there any surprises? What are your conjectures? Is there anything you can be sure about? Why?

The number of vertical edges is equal to the number of horizontal edges. This is true of a rectangle, the simplest rectilinear shape, and any rectilinear alteration can be viewed as converting a portion of a horizontal line segment into two horizontal line segments, and one extra vertical line segment will be needed, preserving the equality in the number of horizontal and vertical line segments. (Alternatively, you could be exchanging a vertical line segment for two vertical line segments and adding one horizontal line segment between them.)

If there are s (smaller) 90° angles and l (larger) 270° angles in a rectilinear n-gon, then $n = s + l$. But the total interior angle must be $180(n - 2)°$, so $90s + 270l = 180(n - 2)$, and since $l = n - s$, $90s + 270(n - s) = 180(n - 2)$. Simplifying, $s + 3n - 3s = 2n - 4$, so $n = 2s - 4$. Since $n = s + l$, then $s + l = 2s - 4$, so $l = s - 4$. So the number of 90° angles is always 4 more than the number of 270° angles – the simplest example being a rectangle, in which $s = 4$ and $l = 0$. (This equation also illustrates why $s \geq 4$, since l cannot be negative.) It can also be seen that 'denting' a vertex from

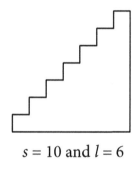

to

exchanges *one* 90° angle for *two* 90° angles and *one* 270° angle, i.e. increases both s and l by 1, leaving the difference, $s - l = 4$, unchanged.

Homework (5 minutes)

Learners could explore the different possible rectilinear shapes that can be drawn for any particular specified pair of (s, l) values. For example, *given that s = 10 and l = 6, what possible rectilinear shapes can be drawn? Do you consider some simpler than others? Why/why not?*

Depending on how learners think about this, they might regard a shape such as this as 'simple' and the basis for others:

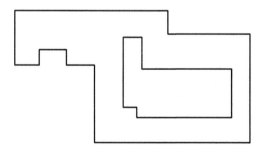

$$s = 10 \text{ and } l = 6$$

To make it harder

Confident learners could consider the situation where the shape has one or more *holes*.

How will you count the angles produced? What if there are 'holes within holes'? They could also look at expressions for the *perimeter* of rectilinear shapes.

To make it easier

The obvious way to begin is with a rectangle, the simplest rectilinear shape, and then try modifying this, by 'denting' a corner:

Rectilinear Shapes

Make some closed polygons using as many line segments as you like but only in these two directions:

vertical   horizontal

For example, you could draw this shape:

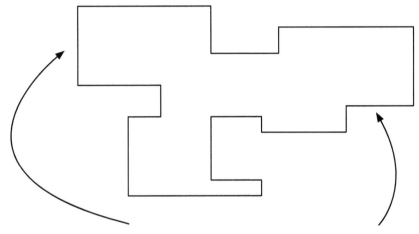

Count the number of vertical line segments and the number of horizontal line segments in this shape and in your shapes.

How are these numbers connected? Why do you think this is?

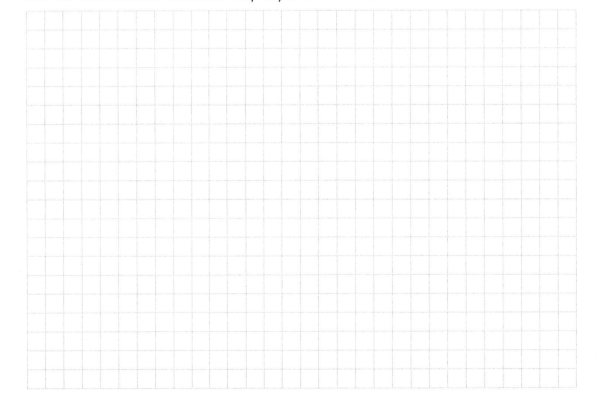

Rectilinear shapes contain two types of interior angle:

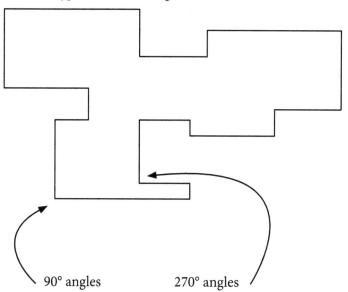

90° angles   270° angles

Count the number of each of these types of interior angle in this shape and in your shapes.
How are these numbers connected? Why do you think this is?

27

Regular Polygons

Introduction

Necessary and sufficient conditions can lead to a lot of confusion in mathematics. An example that is met early on is the definition of a *regular* polygon as one with all equal-length sides (*equilateral*) *and* all equal-angles (*equiangular*). Either condition alone is *necessary*, but only together are they *sufficient* to guarantee that you have a regular polygon:

regular $\Rightarrow$ equilateral   equilateral $\nRightarrow$ regular

regular $\Rightarrow$ equiangular   equiangular $\nRightarrow$ regular

equilateral + equiangular $\Rightarrow$ regular

In this lesson, learners explore various possible polygons and place them in the correct regions of a Venn diagram. Not only is this helpful in appreciating the definition of regular, but also it encourages learners to explore the 'range of permissible change' within the definitions of equilateral and equiangular – the extent to which a polygon can be varied without breaking those conditions.

Aims and outcomes

- Construct polygons according to specified constraints.
- Understand the properties of regular polygons.

Lesson starter (10 minutes)

What do you think a regular *polygon is?*

Learners might give definitions or examples. The word 'regular' means 'ordinary' in 'ordinary' life, and some learners may think that it means 'small' because of its common use in fast food establishments (a 'regular cola' is the smallest available). So they may think that any shape with a familiar name, such as a rectangle, is a regular shape. They may not appreciate that 'regular' has the dual conditions of being equilateral and equiangular: either condition alone is insufficient. It would be best to avoid giving examples at this stage to illustrate this, since that is the purpose of the main lesson.

Main lesson (30 minutes)

Learners will need to know the meanings of the terms *equiangular* (all interior angles equal) and *equilateral* (all sides the same length). They will also need to know that triangles, quadrilaterals, pentagons, hexagons and heptagons are polygons with 3, 4, 5, 6 and 7 sides respectively. Give out the Task Sheets, preferably enlarged onto A3 paper, and encourage learners to experiment with drawing shapes that will go in the various regions.

Plenary (15 minutes)

How did you get on – was it easy or hard? Why?

Were there any regions for which you couldn't find any shapes? Which ones? Why not?

For a triangle, either condition alone, equiangular or equilateral, implies the other, and therefore implies regularity. So the only regions that can contain triangles are the 'outside' and the 'overlap'. However, for all other polygons it is possible to find shapes to go in any of the four regions, although learners may initially think that some are impossible! Possible answers are shown for pentagons and hexagons below, with the shapes drawn accurately.

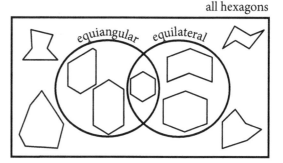

Depending on whether learners accept 'crossed polygons' as polygons, a regular pentagon could be the usual convex kind or the concave star polygon, the *pentagram*. Equiangular but irregular pentagons can be formed by beginning with a regular pentagon and sliding some or all of the sides parallel to themselves. There are many possible equilateral pentagons which are not regular, e.g. two possible versions, each with two right angles, are shown above. Equiangular quadrilaterals are rectangles, while equilateral quadrilaterals are rhombuses; the intersection is the squares. For hexagons, equilaterals must have opposite sides parallel. This is also true of equiangular hexagons, but in this case they need not be equal in length; in fact, the *difference* between the lengths of opposite sides must be equal. (For some lovely proofs, see Ball, D. (2002) 'Equiangular Polygons', *The Mathematical Gazette*, 86, (507), 396–407.)

Homework (5 minutes)

Suppose that you are allowed to use lines of two different lengths only.

What kinds of polygons can you make?

With triangles, you can make isosceles triangles; with quadrilaterals you can make oblongs or non-rhombus kites, etc.

Learners could also be asked to find everyday examples of dual conditions, which must *both* be satisfied for something to be true. For example, in law theft involves *both* taking someone else's property without their permission (*actus reus*) *and* an intention to do so (*mens rea*), so just having the intention, or taking something that you genuinely thought was yours, would not be classified as theft.

To make it harder

Confident learners could explore what happens with polygons in *three* dimensions. Here you can have equilateral, equiangular shapes that are non-planar. A famous example in chemistry is the shape of the molecule cyclohexane:

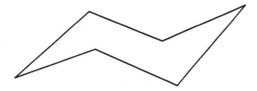

Each vertex represents a carbon atom – the hydrogen atoms are not shown. This is known as the *chair conformation* of cyclohexane; all its angles are 109.5°, which is the most natural angle for four bonds leaving a carbon atom.

To make it easier

Learners who find this hard could start with quadrilaterals and think about what changes as a shape moves around the Venn diagram, crossing the boundaries between the different regions. Straws and Blu-Tack may be useful to assist visualization.

Regular Polygons

There are four regions in each of the Venn diagrams below.

Sketch some shapes to go in as many of the regions as possible.
Do you think any regions are impossible? Why?

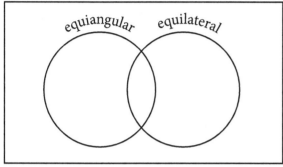

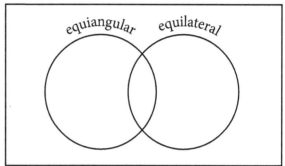

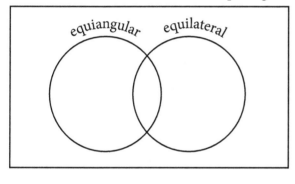

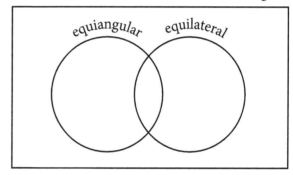

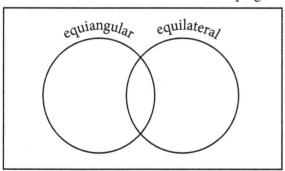

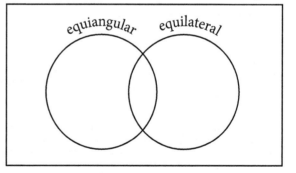

28

Seven Divided by Three

Introduction

The task in this lesson sounds deceptively simple, yet leads to some very interesting mathematics. Sharing out sweets when the number of people is not a factor of the number of sweets leads to either a remainder (sweets left over) or unequal shares. These two possibilities are explored in this lesson, leading to work on partitioning the integers, and a surprising sequence that begins 1, 2, 3, 4, 5, . . . but then the next term is not 6!

Aims and outcomes

- Find all the ways of partitioning a positive integer.
- Round numbers in ways appropriate to different situations.

Lesson starter (10 minutes)

What is 7 divided by 3? Try to think of more than one way of answering this question.

Learners might say 'seven thirds' or 'two and a third' or 'two point three recurring' or 'about two' or 'two and a bit' or 'two remainder one' or 'you can't'.

Try to think of a situation where each answer would be appropriate.

Some possibilities would be:

Possible question	Possible answer
If three people enter a building every minute, how long will it take for seven people to come in?	Around 2 minutes
A newspaper pays me £1 for every three words I write. How much do you think I will get for a 7-word sentence?	I will get £2 (no rounding up, unfortunately!)
I want to divide a 7-metre length of cloth into three equal lengths. How long will each piece be?	Each piece will be $2\frac{1}{3}$ metres or 233 cm (correct to the nearest cm)
Seven pupils must get into groups of three. How many groups of three will there be?	Two groups, with one person left over
If I need seven spoons and they come only in packs of three, how many packs will I have to buy?	Three packs, and I will have two spare spoons

Main lesson (30 minutes)

Suppose we are sharing out 7 sweets among 3 people, and you can't split up a sweet – they have to stay whole. How can you do it?

If you have three groups of 2 and one left over, then that's really *four* groups, so that won't do – think again. Learners will have to make *unequal* groups; somebody has to get an extra one, at least. Give out the Task Sheets and encourage learners to think hard about this problem.

Plenary (15 minutes)

What did you find out? How many ways did you get? Can you convince us that your answer is correct?

The numbers in the table below assume that the three people are distinguishable – for example, (1, 1, 5) is a different distribution of sweets from (1, 5, 1) – but the *sweets* are indistinguishable (identical) – so (1, 1, 5), for instance, is the same no matter which five sweets person C gets. If learners consider the people to be as indistinguishable as the sweets, then there are 4 ways rather than 15 ways.

Partitioning	Person A	Person B	Person C
1 + 1 + 5	1	1	5
	1	5	1
	5	1	1
1 + 2 + 4	1	2	4
	1	4	2
	2	1	4
	2	4	1
	4	1	2
	4	2	1
1 + 3 + 3	1	3	3
	3	1	3
	3	3	1
2 + 2 + 3	2	2	3
	2	3	2
	3	2	2

The 15 ways shown in the table can be thought of as resulting from breaking a chain of 7 sweets in two places (the number of people minus 1), so as to create three groups.

For example: 2 + 2 + 3

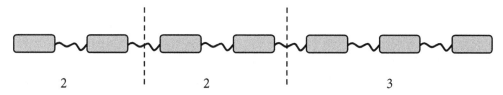

With n sweets and r people, there will be $(n - 1)$ links, $(r - 1)$ of which need to be broken, so there will be $^{n-1}C_{r-1} = \dfrac{(n - 1)!}{(n - r - 2)!(r - 1)!}$ ways of doing it.

When $n = 7$ and $r = 3$, this gives $^6C_2 = 15$. If learners explore different numbers of sweets, they will obtain the following results:

Number of sweets, n	Ways of sharing them among 3 people	*Total number* of ways of sharing them among 3 people
4	(1, 1, 2)	1
5	(1, 1, 3), (1, 2, 2)	2
6	(1, 1, 4), (1, 2, 3), (2, 2, 2)	3
7	(1, 1, 5), (1, 2, 4), (1, 3, 3), (2, 2, 3)	4
8	(1, 1, 6), (1, 2, 5), (1, 3, 4), (2, 2, 4), (2, 3, 3)	5

However, the pattern does not continue going up in 1s. With three sweets, there would be one way of sharing them (1, 1, 1), which suggests that the sequence may be more complicated, since it begins 1, 1, 2, 3, 4, 5, . . . rather than 0, 1, 2, 3, 4, 5, . . . In fact, the next term is 7 rather than 6, and the sequence follows the formula $\left[\dfrac{n^2}{12}\right]$, where the brackets indicate rounding to the nearest integer. In general, if $P(n, r)$ is the number of ways of partitioning n objects in to r subsets, then $P(n, r) = P(n - 1, r - 1) + P(n - r, r)$. So the table would be as follows:

		1	2	3	4	5	6	7	8	9	10	11	12	13	14	15	16	17	18	19	20
	1	1	0	0	0	0	0	0	0	0	0	0	0	0	0	0	0	0	0	0	0
	2	1	1	0	0	0	0	0	0	0	0	0	0	0	0	0	0	0	0	0	0
	3	1	1	1	0	0	0	0	0	0	0	0	0	0	0	0	0	0	0	0	0
	4	1	2	1	1	0	0	0	0	0	0	0	0	0	0	0	0	0	0	0	0
	5	1	2	2	1	1	0	0	0	0	0	0	0	0	0	0	0	0	0	0	0
	6	1	3	3	2	1	1	0	0	0	0	0	0	0	0	0	0	0	0	0	0
	7	1	3	4	3	2	1	1	0	0	0	0	0	0	0	0	0	0	0	0	0
	8	1	4	5	5	3	2	1	1	0	0	0	0	0	0	0	0	0	0	0	0
	9	1	4	7	6	5	3	2	1	1	0	0	0	0	0	0	0	0	0	0	0
n	10	1	5	8	9	7	5	3	2	1	1	0	0	0	0	0	0	0	0	0	0
	11	1	5	10	11	10	7	5	3	2	1	1	0	0	0	0	0	0	0	0	0
	12	1	6	12	15	13	11	7	5	3	2	1	1	0	0	0	0	0	0	0	0
	13	1	6	14	18	18	14	11	7	5	3	2	1	1	0	0	0	0	0	0	0
	14	1	7	16	23	23	20	15	11	7	5	3	2	1	1	0	0	0	0	0	0
	15	1	7	19	27	30	26	21	15	11	7	5	3	2	1	1	0	0	0	0	0
	16	1	8	21	34	37	35	28	22	15	11	7	5	3	2	1	1	0	0	0	0
	17	1	8	24	39	47	44	38	29	22	15	11	7	5	3	2	1	1	0	0	0
	18	1	9	27	47	57	58	49	40	30	22	15	11	7	5	3	2	1	1	0	0
	19	1	9	30	54	70	71	65	52	41	30	22	15	11	7	5	3	2	1	1	0
	20	1	10	33	64	84	90	82	70	54	42	30	22	15	11	7	5	3	2	1	1

(Column group header: r)

Homework (5 minutes)

Decide whether you think this statement is true or false, and say why: 'Every odd number is the sum of a power of 2 and a prime number.'

This appears to work for most odd numbers you try, so learners are very likely to return saying that they think it is true, but in fact the statement is false. Camille Armand Jules Marie, also known as Prince de Polignac (1832–1913), conjectured this, but it fails first with 127, which is 2 + 125 or 4 + 123 or 8 + 119 or 16 + 111 or 32 + 95 or 64 + 63, and none of 125, 123, 119, 111, 95 or 63 is prime. Numbers such as 127, 149, 251, 331, . . . (there are infinitely many) which are counter-examples to the conjecture are sometimes called *Polignac numbers*, or *obstinate numbers*. This provides an example of why a conjecture should not be believed just because you have checked the first hundred or so cases!

To make it harder

Keen learners could find out about or invent other 'surprise sequences', whose beginning suggests one pattern but then which then go on to do something unexpected.

To make it easier

Learners who find this difficult could use cubes to represent the sweets and place them on different pieces of paper to represent the people. They might also benefit from someone else recording the results in an orderly manner.

Seven divided by three

How can you share 7 identical sweets among 3 people?

You have to use all the sweets and you can't split sweets into smaller pieces.

How many different ways are there of doing it?

What if you have a different number of sweets?

What if you have a different number of people?

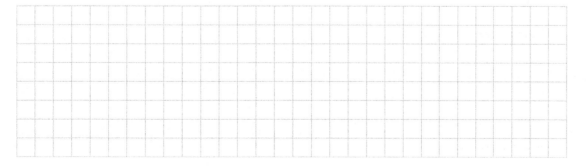

29

Shape Riddles

Introduction

Inclusive definitions (e.g. all squares are rectangles) often create problems for learners. The idea that one category can lie completely within another (i.e. be a subset of it) and yet form only part of it can be difficult to understand. The purpose of inclusive definitions is that, for example, many properties of rectangles in general are also shared by squares (e.g. the formula for the area). By this logic, equilateral triangles might be considered to be special cases of isosceles triangles, and all triangles could even be seen as special cases of trapeziums (with one of the 'parallel' sides shrinking to zero length). However, symmetry properties, typically, are not shared; e.g. a square has diagonal lines of symmetry and order 4 rotational symmetry, whereas non-square rectangles (oblongs) don't have diagonal lines of symmetry and have order of rotational symmetry of only 2. Although we might think of equilateral triangles as a subset of isosceles triangles, we would not think of isosceles triangles as a subset of scalene triangles.

Aims and outcomes

- Classify quadrilaterals according to their properties.
- Understand the nature of inclusive definitions.

Lesson starter (10 minutes)

Display this sentence on the board as learners enter the room:

> A *blank* is always a *blank-blank*, but a *blank-blank* is not necessarily a *blank*, because it could be a *blank-blank-blank*.

They will probably be mystified by it.

Without explaining, point at the words as written but say something like: 'A *dog* is always an *animal*, but an *animal* is not necessarily a *dog*, because it could be a *cat*.'

Perhaps give another example (e.g. an 8FR-er [or whatever your class is called], member of Year 8 [or whatever Year group they are in], 8ML-er [some other form group in the Year]) and then ask learners to say examples out loud. Once a significant proportion of the class are accepting the idea, ask for *mathematical* examples. For instance, you could have (integer, number, 'decimal'), (triangle, shape, square) or (prime number greater than 2, odd number, odd multiple of 9).

Main lesson (30 minutes)

Have you heard this riddle? 'When is a door not a door?' When it's a-jar! Can you explain it?

Give out the Task Sheets – the questions sound a bit like this kind of joke, but can be answered by thinking about what properties are necessary for a shape to have in order to be given a certain name. Encourage learners to complete the sheet, explaining exactly what they mean for each one.

Plenary (15 minutes)

How did you get on? Which ones did you find hardest? Were there any you weren't sure about? Why?

Possible answers are:

- When is a *rectangle* not a *square*? When its sides are not all the same length; or when it's an oblong.
- When is a *parallelogram* not a *square*? When its sides are not the same length and/or at least one of its angles is not 90° (which implies that none of them is).
- When is a *rhombus* not a *square*? When at least one of its angles is not 90° (which implies that none of them is).
- When is a *parallelogram* not a *rhombus*? When its sides are not all the same length.
- When is a *parallelogram* not a *rectangle*? When at least one of its angles is not 90° (which implies that none of them is).
- When is a *polygon* not a *pentagon*? When it has more or fewer sides than 5.
- When is a *polygon* not a *quadrilateral*? When it has more or fewer sides than 4.

Homework (5 minutes)

Learners could try to apply this sort of approach to other areas in mathematics; for example, numbers: 'An even number is always an integer but an integer is not necessarily an even number because it could be odd.' They could be asked to write down six of these, each from a different area of mathematics.

To make it harder

Learners confident with this work could consider logical fallacies such as: 'All cows eat grass; Daisy eats grass; Therefore Daisy is a cow', perhaps exposing the error by drawing a Venn diagram in which cows are a subset of 'grass-eaters' but where Daisy could be, for example, a sheep (with a confusingly cow-like name!). It is easy to see from Venn diagrams why 'All cows eat grass; Daisy is a cow; Therefore Daisy eats grass', on the other hand, *does* represent correct logic.

To make it easier

Learners could try to make a diagram (perhaps a Venn diagram) summarizing some of the inclusive definitions; for example, for quadrilaterals. For a nice possibility, see Ling, J. (2001) 'Classifying Quadrilaterals', *Mathematics in School*, 30, (1), 40.

Shape Riddles

Fill in the gaps below.

You can describe shapes by using their names or by saying their properties.

When is a *rectangle* not a *square*? When it's	When is a *square* not a *rectangle*? Never!
When is a *parallelogram* not a *square*? When it's	When is a *square* not a *parallelogram*? Never!
When is a *rhombus* not a *square*? When it's	When is a *square* not a *rhombus*? Never!
When is a *parallelogram* not a *rhombus*? When it's	When is a *rhombus* not a *parallelogram*? Never!
When is a *parallelogram* not a *rectangle*? When it's	When is a *rectangle* not a *parallelogram*? Never!
When is a *polygon* not a *pentagon*? When it's	When is a *pentagon* not a *polygon*? Never!
When is a *polygon* not a *quadrilateral*? When it's	When is a *quadrilateral* not a *polygon*? Never!

© Colin Foster (2011) *Resources for Teaching Mathematics 11–14*. London: Continuum

Make up some more like these.

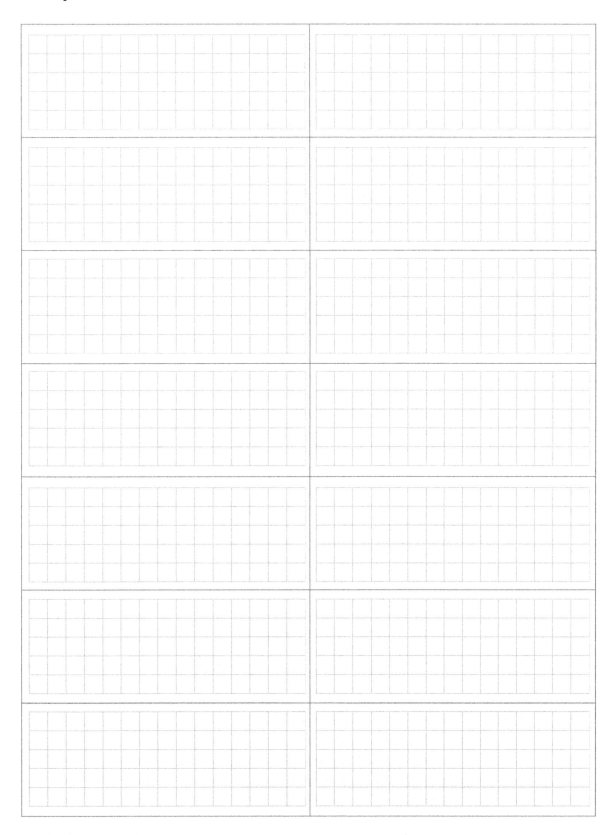

30

Shapes within Shapes

Introduction

This lesson starts with some simple-looking geometrical patterns and gives learners the freedom to focus on any aspect of the pattern, counting line segments, vertices or any shapes that they can trace out within the drawings. In each case, different patterns will be found. In the notes below, some quite complicated formulae are given, for the teacher's convenience – it is not expected that all learners will find all of these, but they will hopefully appreciate something of the richness of the mathematical structure embedded in these geometrical designs.

Aims and outcomes

- Explain numerical patterns in terms of geometrical features.
- Find numerical sequences from geometrical drawings.
- Find patterns in sequences and describe them using formulae.

Lesson starter (10 minutes)

How many triangles are there in this drawing.

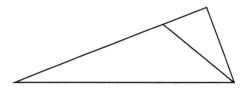

If someone says 'two', ask them to describe or point to the ones they see. *Does anyone see any more?*

There are three:

Then add further line segments, zigzagging through the large triangle:

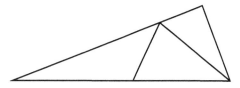   then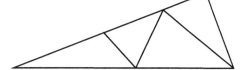

How many now? How many now?

The sequence goes 3, 5, 7, 9, . . ., increasing by 2 each time.

Can you explain why it goes up in 2s?

Every extra line segment creates two extra small triangles, increasing the total number of triangles by 2. So the nth drawing will have $2n + 1$ triangles.

Main lesson (30 minutes)

Give out the Task Sheets and encourage learners to choose something to count and see what patterns they can discover.

Plenary (15 minutes)

What did you find? Did anyone find triangle numbers? Square numbers? Any other kinds of numbers? Where? How?

Triangles

There are many patterns to be found, depending on what learners choose to count. The total number of 'point-up' and 'point-down' triangles are given in the table below.

Shape number, n	Number of 'point-up' triangles, u	Number of 'point-down' triangles, d	Total number of triangles, $t = u + d$
1	1	0	1
2	4 = 3 + 1	1	5
3	10 = 6 + 3 + 1	3	13
4	20 = 10 + 6 + 3 + 1	7 = 6 + 1	27
5	35 = 15 + 10 + 6 + 3 + 1	13 = 10 + 3	48
6	56 = 21 + 15 + 10 + 6 + 3 + 1	22 = 15 + 6 + 1	78

The total number of *smallest* 'point-up' triangles is the nth *triangle number*, $\frac{1}{2}n(n + 1)$; the total number of smallest 'point-down' triangles is the $(n - 1)$th *triangle number*, $\frac{1}{2}n(n - 1)$; the total number of *all* the smallest triangles is the sum of these, the nth *square number*, n^2.

The total number of 'point-up' triangles of any size, u_n, is the nth *tetrahedral number* (the sum of the first n triangle numbers). So $u_n = {}^{n+2}C_3 = \frac{1}{6}n(n + 1)(n + 2)$. However, the total number of 'point-down' triangles, d_n, is more difficult. It is the sum of the *alternate* triangle numbers up to the $(n - 1)$th, and this sum is $d_n = \left\lfloor \frac{1}{24}n(n + 2)(2n - 1) \right\rfloor$, where the square brackets indicate rounding down, since although the formula is exact when n is even, it gives the required integer plus $\frac{1}{8}$ over when n is odd. (Alternatively you could use this formula for even n and have the same formula, subtract $\frac{1}{8}$, for odd n.) So the total number of triangles, t_n, can be written as $t_n = \left\lfloor \frac{1}{8}n(n + 2)(2n + 1) \right\rfloor$.

Learners who envisage the shapes as made of 'matchsticks' and count the matchsticks will find that the total number of sticks is three times the number of smallest point-up triangles; i.e. $\frac{3}{2}n(n + 1)$. Learners could also count trapeziums (which are $(n - 1)(2n - 1)$), rhombuses (which are the centred triangle numbers, $\frac{1}{2}(3n(n - 1) + 2)$) and parallelograms (which are $\frac{1}{2}(n - 1)n(n + 1)$). (These results are for counting the *smallest* possible version of each of these shapes.)

Squares

An $n \times n$ square obviously contains n^2 one-by-one squares. The total number of squares of *any* size is the sum of the first n square numbers, which is $\frac{1}{6}n(n + 1)(2n + 1)$.

The total number of rectangles is the sum of the first n cube numbers, which is $\frac{1}{4}n^2(n + 1)^2$.

Hexagons

The number of small hexagons in the nth drawing is the nth centred hexagonal number (also called *hex numbers*), 1, 7, 19, 37, . . ., given by the formula $3n^2 - 3n + 1$. Another way of writing this is as $n^3 - (n - 1)^3$, and this version of the formula can be seen geometrically if learners can envisage the drawing three-dimensionally. (Some may do this spontaneously when they first look at it.) In the drawing shown over the page, where $n = 3$, we can consider that we are looking at the outer layer of a $3 \times 3 \times 3$ cube of hexagons, and the number of hexagons that we can see must be $3^3 - 2^3$, since there is a $2 \times 2 \times 2$ cube inside that we cannot see.

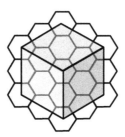

Homework (5 minutes)

Learners could be asked to investigate further sequences of these kinds at home. Alternatively, they could explore *The On-Line Encyclopedia of Integer Sequences* (at www.research.att.com/~njas/ sequences/) and find three interesting sequences that they didn't previously know about and which they can describe and explain next lesson.

To make it harder

There should be plenty here for all learners to explore, particularly when examining multiple copies of more complicated shapes found within the diagrams.

To make it easier

Learners who find this hard could begin by counting all the small triangles only – they may be surprised to find the *square* numbers rather than triangle numbers.

Shapes within Shapes

How many triangles are there in each drawing? There may be more than you think.

What other things can you count in these drawings?
What patterns can you find? Can you explain them?

How many squares are there in each drawing? Why?
How many rectangles? Why?

What can you count in these drawings?

Make other sequences of drawings.
What patterns can you find and explain?

© Colin Foster (2011)   *Resources for Teaching Mathematics 11–14*. London: Continuum

31

Sharing Camels

Introduction

This is an ancient problem that appears from time to time in various guises. It is not intended to be a realistic practical problem – on the contrary, it is merely a recreational amusement – but is used in this lesson to engage learners in thinking about proportions and ratio. The issue of fairness pushes learners into taking a position on what they think about the events of the story.

Aims and outcomes

- Add and subtract fractions.
- Share amounts in a specified ratio.
- Understand and use remainders when dividing.

Lesson starter (15 minutes)

Here is a puzzle that learners may have heard before:

A wealthy man dies and leaves all his camels to his three sons, saying in his will that he wants $\frac{1}{2}$ of them to go to his eldest son, $\frac{1}{4}$ to the middle son and $\frac{1}{5}$ to the youngest. When he dies, he leaves 19 camels, which causes a problem – why?

None of the amounts is a whole numbers of camels. (Also, learners may notice that the three fractions do not add up to 1.)

How many camels would work?

Any even number would be OK for the first son, any multiple of four would be OK for the middle son and any multiple of 5 would be OK for the youngest son, but to be OK for all of them requires any multiple of the lowest common multiple of 2, 4 and 5; i.e. any multiple of 20.

Main lesson (25 minutes)

Give out the Task Sheets. You could read together the end of the story, if you wish. Then encourage learners to think about the questions.

Plenary (15 minutes)

How many camels did each son get?

The numbers are shown in the table below:

Son	Number of camels
1	$\frac{1}{2} \times 20 = 10$
2	$\frac{1}{4} \times 20 = 5$
3	$\frac{1}{5} \times 20 = 4$
Total	19

This left one camel, which, of course, they returned to the wise woman (it was the one they borrowed from her in the first place). So it was fair to the wise old woman, in the sense that she got her camel back, although neither she nor her camel got anything for their trouble! It is probably 'fair' to say that it was unfair to *everyone else*. The father did not specify how to allocate all of his property, since $\frac{1}{2} + \frac{1}{4} + \frac{1}{5} = \frac{19}{20} < 1$, so each son obtained more than the father intended, since they all obtained their fraction *of 20* rather than *of 19*. So they each got $\frac{20}{19}$ of what they should have done. This means that the eldest son gained the most, since he was getting the most anyway. The unallocated $\frac{1}{20}$ of the 19 camels was divided among the three sons in the same ratio that the father specified for the $\frac{19}{20}$ of the 19 camels.

If we assume that the father stipulates *unit fractions* (i.e. fractions with a numerator of 1, when written in their simplest form), then this sort of situation will be possible only when we have three unit fractions that add up to a fraction of the form $\frac{n-1}{n}$, where n is a positive integer. This is a unit fraction less than 1, since $\frac{n-1}{n} = 1 - \frac{1}{n}$, meaning that the problem reduces to seeking four unit fractions that add up to 1, the three smallest of which must be distinct. The first son must always take $\frac{1}{2}$, since it is impossible to reach 1 otherwise, with only three sons, since $\frac{1}{3} + \frac{1}{4} + \frac{1}{5} + \frac{1}{6} = \frac{19}{20}$.

The only ways of writing 1 as the sum of four unit fractions, with the first three distinct, are the following eight.

$$\frac{1}{2} + \frac{1}{3} + \frac{1}{7} + \frac{1}{42} = 1 \qquad \frac{1}{2} + \frac{1}{3} + \frac{1}{12} + \frac{1}{12} = 1$$

$$\frac{1}{2} + \frac{1}{3} + \frac{1}{8} + \frac{1}{24} = 1 \qquad \frac{1}{2} + \frac{1}{4} + \frac{1}{5} + \frac{1}{20} = 1$$

$$\frac{1}{2} + \frac{1}{3} + \frac{1}{9} + \frac{1}{18} = 1 \qquad \frac{1}{2} + \frac{1}{4} + \frac{1}{6} + \frac{1}{12} = 1$$

$$\frac{1}{2} + \frac{1}{3} + \frac{1}{10} + \frac{1}{15} = 1 \qquad \frac{1}{2} + \frac{1}{4} + \frac{1}{8} + \frac{1}{8} = 1$$

These correspond, respectively, to the seven solutions below ($\frac{1}{2} + \frac{1}{3} + \frac{1}{10} + \frac{1}{15} = 1$ has to be omitted, since the denominator of the final fraction is odd).

Number of camels left by father	Fractions
41	$\frac{1}{2}, \frac{1}{3}, \frac{1}{7}$
23	$\frac{1}{2}, \frac{1}{3}, \frac{1}{8}$
17	$\frac{1}{2}, \frac{1}{3}, \frac{1}{9}$
11	$\frac{1}{2}, \frac{1}{3}, \frac{1}{12}$
19	$\frac{1}{2}, \frac{1}{4}, \frac{1}{5}$
11	$\frac{1}{2}, \frac{1}{4}, \frac{1}{6}$
7	$\frac{1}{2}, \frac{1}{4}, \frac{1}{8}$

Learners may be surprised that no more solutions are possible, unless the wise woman has more camels!

Homework (5 minutes)

Find out about *Egyptian Fractions*. Learners could perhaps make a poster illustrating what they are and how they work.

To make it harder

Allowing more than one camel to be borrowed would complicate the situation in an interesting way for anyone very confident with these ideas.

To make it easier

Learners who find this hard might benefit from some identical objects (e.g. cubes) to aid visualization.

Nineteen Camels

A wealthy man dies and leaves all his camels to his three sons, saying in his will that he wants $\frac{1}{2}$ of them to go to his eldest son, $\frac{1}{4}$ to the middle son and $\frac{1}{5}$ to the youngest.

When he dies, he leaves 19 camels, which causes a problem.

The three sons go to ask a wise old woman what to do.

She solves it this way: she lends them her camel, temporarily, so that they have 20 altogether. So they work it out with 20 instead of 19.

Why is this easier?

How many camels did each son get? Why?

How many camels were left over? Why?

Do you think this was fair? Why/why not?

Make up other camel problems like this, where borrowing *just one camel* is enough to sort out the problem.

Explain how to choose the numbers for camel problems like this.

32

Simultaneous Investigation

Introduction

In this lesson, learners generate for themselves a lot of practice at solving pairs of linear simultaneous equations while pursuing (simultaneously!) an interesting investigation. Restricting the solutions to integers introduces a constraint that gives learners plenty to ponder. Equations with integer solutions are known as *Diophantine equations*.

Aims and outcomes

- Solve linear simultaneous equations in two unknowns.
- Substitute into algebraic expressions to find integer solutions.

Lesson starter (10 minutes)

Look at these simultaneous equations:

$$2x + 3y = \square$$
$$3x + 2y = \square$$

Make up numbers to go in the boxes so that x *and* y *are integers. The two boxes don't have to be the same number.*

(But *can* they be the same number? Learners might consider this.)

Learners can construct their equations by beginning with possible integer values for x and y – they could choose quite difficult values, and in this way end up with challenging simultaneous equations. Then learners could demonstrate the solution of the their equations, either 'by inspection' (i.e. by 'knowing' the answer!) or by an algebraic method.

The only way the two boxes can be equal is if $x = y$; most obviously, perhaps, in the cases where $x = y = 0$ or $x = y = 1$.

Main lesson (30 minutes)

Give out the Task Sheets and encourage learners to explore the possibilities with different box numbers.

Plenary (15 minutes)

What did you find out about what numbers can go in the box?

The given equations together imply that $3x = \square - 5$, so $3x + 5 = \square$ or $3(x + 1) + 2 = \square$, meaning that the box must be two more than a multiple of 3. For positive values of x and y, we have only the following possibilities:

x	y	$\square = 3n + 2$, where n is an integer $2 \leq n \leq 5$
1	4	8
2	3	11
3	2	14
4	1	17

With the same first equation and $ax + y = \square$ (where a is positive integer greater than 1) as the second equation, we can have box numbers equal to $a + 4$, $2a + 3$, $3a + 2$ and $4a + 1$, so there are still four possible box numbers, whatever value of a we choose, given by $(a - 1)n + 5$, for integer $1 \leq n \leq 4$. For instance, if $a = 2$ then the box number can be 6, 7, 8 or 9.

Homework (5 minutes)

Learners could do the same thing with the pair of equations:

$$x + y = 5$$
$$2x - y = \square$$

Find all the possible positive integer values that the box can have, if x *and* y *are also positive integers.*

There are only four pairs of possible values of x and y, if both are positive integers:

x	y	Box
1	4	Impossible (−2)
2	3	1
3	2	4
4	1	7

However, when $x = 1$ the box number would be negative, so there are just three possible box number values: 1, 4 and 7.

To make it harder

Confident learners could introduce a second box somewhere in the first equation and make a two-way table of possibilities.

To make it easier

Learners who find this difficult could initially consider the possibilities of the first equation, if x and y have to be positive integers, recording the possible values of x and y in a table. Then they could change the '5' (the constant term) to another number and repeat the process. If the constant term is n, there are $(n - 1)$ pairs of possible values of x and y.

Simultaneous Investigation

For these simultaneous equations, what values can you put in the box so that *both* solutions (x and y) are integers? Why?

$$x + y = 5$$

$$4x + y = \square$$

What if x and y have to be *positive* integers?

Try changing the '4' in the second equation to something else. What difference does this make?

Make up other pairs of simultaneous equations where there is one box number.

Explore the possible values this box can take if all the solutions must be positive integers.

33 Sinusoids

Introduction

This lesson offers an approach to trigonometry that complements the more common way of beginning by considering right-angled triangles and the ratios of the lengths of their sides. Learners begin with a circle and examine the horizontal and vertical coordinates of points around the edge, leading to the sinusoidal graphs of sin and cos. This 'functional' approach can be helpful for learners who have previously thought of trigonometry as only being about ratios. It could also be an alternative way to begin, with learners seeing a rotating unit length as a hypotenuse and sin as the vertical displacement of its rotating end and cos as the horizontal displacement: all triangles can then be thought of as enlargements of this unit-hypotenuse triangle. It is also useful for considering angles greater than 90°.

Aims and outcomes

- Draw and interpret graphs of trigonometric functions.
- Understand the trigonometric ratios sin, cos and tan.

Lesson starter (10 minutes)

Ask one learner to walk around in a circle, marked out on the floor. Ask two other learners to track the movement in two perpendicular directions, as shown below.

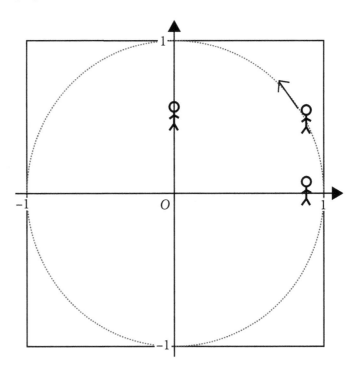

What do you think will happen when we do this? Why?

    The two 'trackers' will move in sinusoidal paths, as sine and cosine functions, but unless learners offer this sort of statement you might prefer to save formal descriptions of this for after the main lesson.

Main lesson (30 minutes)

Give out the Task Sheets and encourage learners, perhaps, to estimate to 1 decimal place. Learners could plot the graphs as they go, which can lead to a more dramatic development. Alternatively, if learners are collecting the numbers in the table first, encourage them to keep their mind on what they are doing, making conjectures about what is going to happen next, looking for surprises, etc., rather than treating it as a mindless 'fill in the gaps' exercise!

Plenary (15 minutes)

What do your graphs look like? Why do you think that is?

Learners may notice that certain points, other than $(0, \pm10)$ and $(\pm10, 0)$, seem to lie exactly on horizontal or vertical grid lines, and in fact they do, since $\sin 30 = \sin 150 = \cos 60 = \cos 300 = \frac{1}{2}$ and $\sin 210 = \sin 330 = \cos 120 = \cos 240 = -\frac{1}{2}$.

Since $x = \cos \theta$ and $y = \sin \theta$, these are the graphs learners should obtain. There may be some discussion about how to connect the points – line segments or a curve. Learners may comment on the fact that continuing to rotate past 360° will reproduce the same graphs again and again, so they are periodic, with period 360°, oscillating continuously between 1 and –1. The sin and cos graphs are identical except for a phase shift of 90°.

Homework (5 minutes)

Find out about natural phenomena that *oscillate*; for example, tides, objects that swing or sway from side to side, such as pendulums, and springs. There are cross-curricular links here with music.

To make it harder

Learners who finish early could work out xy and $\frac{y}{x}$ and plot these against θ.

Since $\frac{y}{x} = \tan\theta$, learners should obtain the $\tan \theta$ graph from this, with asymptotes (and discontinuities) at $\theta = 90° + 180n°$, where n is an integer, since $x = 0$. This graph has half the period of the sin θ and cos θ graphs; only 180°.

Since $xy = \cos \theta \sin \theta = \frac{1}{2}\sin 2\theta$, this should lead to a graph exactly like sin θ but with twice the frequency (a period of 180°, the same as the tan θ graph) and half the amplitude. As the radius of the unit circle rotates anticlockwise, this can be thought of as plotting twice the (signed) area of the right-angled triangle formed by the radius, the x-axis and the y-ordinate. The area would be $\frac{1}{2}\cos \theta \sin \theta = \frac{1}{4}\sin 2\theta$. This has a maximum/minimum in each quadrant where $\theta = \pm 45° + 180n°$, where n is an integer.

To make it easier

Learners who find it hard to estimate the coordinates might find it easier to focus just on the points in the first quadrant (positive x and positive y) initially.

Sinusoids

Estimate as accurately as you can the coordinates of the points marked on the circumference of the circle. Put the values into the tables on the right.

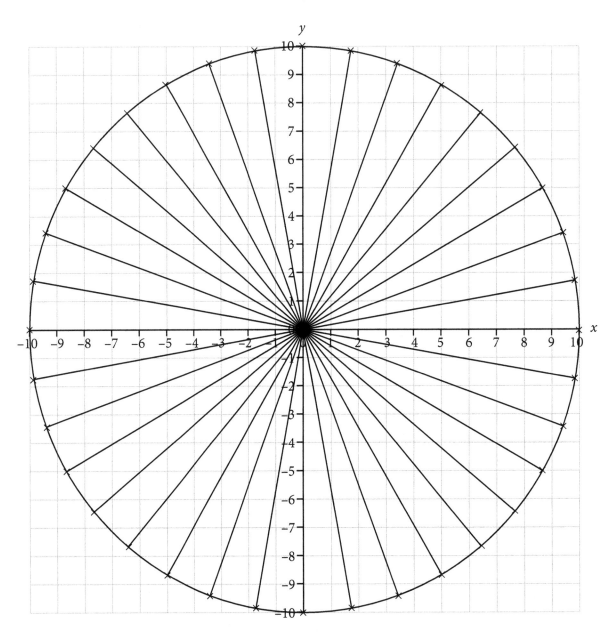

Let θ be the *anticlockwise* angle that each radius makes with the positive x-axis.

θ (°)	0	10	20	30	40	50	60	70	80	90	100	110
x												
y												

θ (°)	120	130	140	150	160	170	180	190	200	210	220	230
x												
y												

θ (°)	240	250	260	270	280	290	300	310	320	330	340	350
x												
y												

What do you notice about the values of x and y?

Draw a graph of x against θ and another graph of y against θ.

Write down what you notice about them.

How are they the same and how are they different?

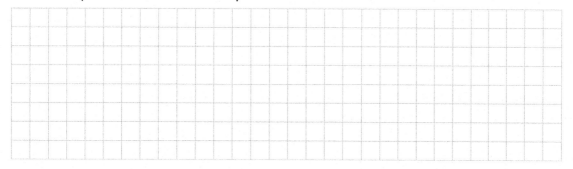

34

Squares and Remainders

Introduction

It is not widely known that square numbers cannot be one less than a multiple of 3, so even mathematics teachers are sometimes surprised by the outcome to the starter of this lesson. Although it might be easier to use modular arithmetic to analyse these processes, this lesson provides an excuse to do some expanding and simplifying of algebraic expressions in order to prove some interesting results. Learners are unlikely to think of expressing the problem in this way unless they have done similar work previously, so this lesson would follow on well from previous lessons relating to algebraic proof.

Aims and outcomes

- Expand pairs of brackets and simplify quadratic expressions.
- Reason algebraically about divisibility and remainders.

Lesson starter (10 minutes)

Think of a positive integer. Don't tell anyone what it is. Divide it by 3. (You might or might not want to allow calculators for this.) *Put your hand up if it divided* exactly, *with no remainder – in other words, you got an integer. Now put up your hand if you had a remainder of 1 – in other words, you got something-and-a-third or something-point-3-recurring. Now put up your hand if you had a remainder of 2 – in other words, you got something-and-*two-*thirds or something-point-6-recurring.*

You will probably get about the same number in each category if your class is large enough. Learners might need help in interpreting 'something-point-6-recurring' on a calculator display as a remainder of 2, etc. One approach is to subtract the integer part and multiply the decimal part by 3.

Now go back to your original number, or you can choose another one if you want, any positive integer. This time square it. (Learners are likely to need calculators – or paper – at this point!) *Now divide it by 3. Put your hand up if it divided exactly, with no remainder. Now put up your hand if you had a remainder of 1. Now put up your hand if you had a remainder of 2.*

This time, if they have done it correctly, *no one* should have a remainder of 2. You may also notice that roughly twice as many people had a remainder of 1 as had a remainder of 0.

Why did that happen?

Encourage learners to think about this in pairs, but you could leave this unresolved and move directly into the main part of the lesson.

Main lesson (30 minutes)

Give out the Task Sheets and encourage learners to try different numbers at the start. They should find that they get remainders of 0 and 1 with equal frequency but no others. Learners are likely to find this surprising and intriguing.

Plenary (15 minutes)

What did you find out? Can you explain what happened with squaring and dividing by 3? Can you explain what happened with squaring and dividing by 4?

Dividing by 3: All integers can be expressed as $3n$, $3n + 1$ or $3n + 2$. If learners choose their integers at random, they should be equally likely to choose each, so remainders of 0, 1 and 2, respectively, will arise. (It would also be possible to write the $3n + 2$ case as $3n - 1$.) However, when squared we obtain $(3n)^2 = 9n^2 = 3(3n^2)$, $(3n + 1)^2 = 9n^2 + 6n + 1 = 3(3n^2 + 2n) + 1$, $(3n + 2)^2 = 9n^2 + 12n + 4 = 3(3n^2 + 4n + 1) + 1$. So the first case leads to no remainder when divided by 3, but the second and third cases *both* lead to a remainder of 1. *None* of the cases leads to a remainder of 2. So it is not possible to get a remainder of 2. Also, we can see why we get twice as many remainders of 1 as remainders of 0.

Dividing by 4: Although 'the same thing' happens with 'divide by 4', the remainders of 0 and 1 are *equally* likely this time. (Again, no other remainders are possible.) This can be proved algebraically in a similar way, by expanding $(4n)^2$, $(4n + 1)^2$, $(4n + 2)^2$ and $(4n + 3)^2$, or by means of 'proofs without words' such as the following:

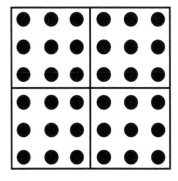 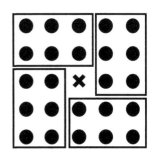

All even squares are (square) multiples of 4; all odd squares are *one more* than a multiple of 4.

Dividing square numbers by other amounts leads to remainders in the proportions shown in this table. (The third row, for instance, shows the results explained above, where there is $\frac{1}{3}$ probability of obtaining no remainder and $\frac{2}{3}$ probability of obtaining a remainder of 1.)

Divide by . . .	Probability of obtaining a remainder of . . .									
	0	1	2	3	4	5	6	7	8	9
1	1	0	0	0	0	0	0	0	0	0
2	$\frac{1}{2}$	$\frac{1}{2}$	0	0	0	0	0	0	0	0
3	$\frac{1}{3}$	$\frac{2}{3}$	0	0	0	0	0	0	0	0
4	$\frac{1}{2}$	$\frac{1}{2}$	0	0	0	0	0	0	0	0
5	$\frac{1}{5}$	$\frac{2}{5}$	0	0	$\frac{2}{5}$	0	0	0	0	0
6	$\frac{1}{6}$	$\frac{1}{3}$	0	$\frac{1}{6}$	$\frac{1}{3}$	0	0	0	0	0
7	$\frac{1}{7}$	$\frac{2}{7}$	$\frac{2}{7}$	0	$\frac{2}{7}$	0	0	0	0	0
8	$\frac{1}{4}$	$\frac{1}{2}$	0	0	$\frac{1}{4}$	0	0	0	0	0
9	$\frac{1}{3}$	$\frac{2}{9}$	0	0	$\frac{2}{9}$	0	0	$\frac{2}{9}$	0	0
10	$\frac{1}{10}$	$\frac{1}{5}$	0	0	$\frac{1}{5}$	$\frac{1}{10}$	$\frac{1}{5}$	0	0	$\frac{1}{5}$

Homework (5 minutes)

Can n^2 be an integer if n isn't an integer? Why/why not?

Can n^2 be a multiple of 5 if n isn't a multiple of 5? Why/why not?

Can n^2 be a multiple of 4 if n isn't a multiple of 4? Why/why not?

No, no, yes. In general n^2 can be a multiple of k, even if n isn't a multiple of k, provided that k itself is a square number, because then n can be a multiple of $\sqrt{k}$.

To make it harder

Keen learners, perhaps with the help of spreadsheet software, could examine what happens with cubes and higher powers. On division by 3, cubes give all three possible remainders in equal proportions. Powers of 4 behave similarly to squares on division by 3 and 4, and learners might like to think why. There is much here to explore.

To make it easier

Learners who find this hard might find that plastic cubes are useful in visualizing both the squares and the remainders on division. They could begin by looking for squares that are exact multiples of 3 and then of 4.

Squares and Remainders

Try following this flow diagram.

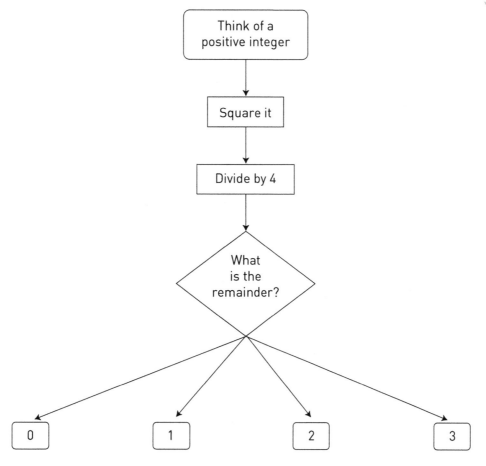

What happens with different numbers?

Which remainders do you get? Do they come equally often?

Which remainders *don't* you get?

Can you explain your results?

Instead of dividing by 4, try dividing by a different number.

Can you explain what happens?

35

Squares and Roots

Introduction

Square numbers have many interesting properties and this lesson seeks to develop learners' familiarity with the squares as preparation for working with surds. Simplifying surds involves isolating and removing square factors; e.g. $\sqrt{72} = \sqrt{36}\sqrt{2} = 6\sqrt{2}$. Choosing, as here, the largest square that is a factor of the number leads to a more rapid and efficient simplification than a longer process such as $\sqrt{72} = \sqrt{9}\sqrt{8} = 3\sqrt{8} = 3\sqrt{4}\sqrt{2} = 6\sqrt{2}$.

Aims and outcomes

- Know and use the square numbers.
- Show equivalence between expressions involving surds.
- Simplify surds.

Lesson starter (10 minutes)

Can you think of a square number? And another one? And another one?

Make a list on the board, perhaps putting them in order.

How many square numbers do you need to add together to make each of the integers from 1 to 20? Try to use as few as possible.

The minimum number of squares needed is shown below, together with an example for each.

n	Minimum number of squares needed to sum to n	Example
1	1	1
2	**2**	**1 + 1**
3	3	1 + 1 + 1
4	1	4
5	**2**	**1 + 4**
6	3	1 + 1 + 4
7	4	1 + 1 + 1 + 4
8	**2**	**4 + 4**
9	1	9
10	**2**	**1 + 9**
11	3	1 + 1 + 9
12	3	4 + 4 + 4
13	**2**	**4 + 9**
14	3	1 + 4 + 9
15	4	1 + 1 + 4 + 9
16	1	16
17	**2**	**1 + 16**
18	**2**	**9 + 9**
19	3	1 + 9 + 9
20	**2**	**4 + 16**

The ones in bold (2, 5, 8, 10, 13, 17, 18, 20, . . .) are the sum of *exactly two* squares.

What other numbers are the sum of two squares?

The sequence continues: 26, 29, 32, 34, 37, 40, 41, 45, . . .

All the answers in the table are 1, 2, 3 or 4. Lagrange's *four-square theorem* says that you can make *any* positive integer by adding up *at most* four squares.

Main lesson (30 minutes)

$\sqrt{2} + \sqrt{8} = \sqrt{18}$ *Do you think that this is true or false? Why?*

Learners could verify this on a calculator, or write:

$$\sqrt{2} + \sqrt{8} = \sqrt{2} + \sqrt{4}\sqrt{2} = \sqrt{2} + 2\sqrt{2} = 3\sqrt{2} = \sqrt{9}\sqrt{2} = \sqrt{18}$$

Why do the numbers 2, 8 and 18 work? Can you find another three numbers that will work? Can you describe all possible *sets of working numbers?*

Give out the Task Sheets and encourage learners to think more about this problem.

Plenary (15 minutes)

What equations did you find? What other examples did you come up with?

Learners may notice the solution $a = b = c = 0$ or, more generally, $a = b$ and $c = 4a$. They also may try working backwards; for example, starting with $\sqrt{3} + 2\sqrt{3} = 3\sqrt{3}$ and obtaining $\sqrt{3} + \sqrt{12} = \sqrt{27}$. This is a good way to obtain examples such as $\sqrt{2} + \sqrt{8} + \sqrt{32} = \sqrt{98}$, by beginning with $\sqrt{2} + 2\sqrt{2} + 4\sqrt{2} = 7\sqrt{2}$.

If $\sqrt{a} + \sqrt{b} = \sqrt{c}$, then $(\sqrt{a} + \sqrt{b})^2 = c$, so $a + \sqrt{a}\sqrt{b} + b = c$, giving $\sqrt{a}\sqrt{b} = c - a - b$, so $\sqrt{ab} = c - a - b$, an integer, meaning that ab must be a perfect square and $c \geq (a + b)$.

One possible question would be whether it is possible to have $\sqrt{a} + \sqrt{b} = \sqrt{ab}$; possible solutions are $a = b = 0$ and $a = b = 4$.

Homework (5 minutes)

Find out what Fermat's Last Theorem *is and who proved it. (It wasn't proved by Fermat!)*

Andrew Wiles (b. 1953) proved the theorem in 1995, after 'nearly' proving it two years before.

What is special about 32 043²?

It is equal to 1 026 753 849, which contains every digit exactly once; i.e. it is the smallest *pan-digital square*.

To make it harder

Confident learners could search for solutions, among the integers, to the equations $a^2 + b^2 = c^2$ (Pythagorean triples) or $a^2 + b^2 = c^2 + d^2$, etc.

To make it easier

Learners who find this hard could begin by finding integer solutions to $\sqrt{a} = b\sqrt{c}$.

Squares and Roots

$$\sqrt{2} + \sqrt{8} = \sqrt{18}$$

Find some more equations like this one.

Find integers a, b and c such that $\sqrt{a} + \sqrt{b} = \sqrt{c}$.

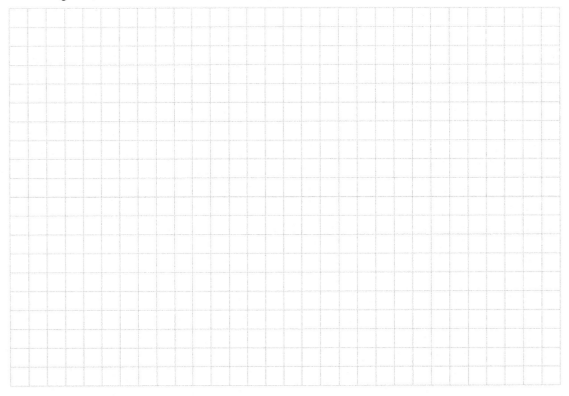

© Colin Foster (2011)   *Resources for Teaching Mathematics 11–14*. London: Continuum

Find integers a, b, c and d such that $\sqrt{a} + \sqrt{b} + \sqrt{c} = \sqrt{d}$.

What other questions can you ask and answer involving surds?

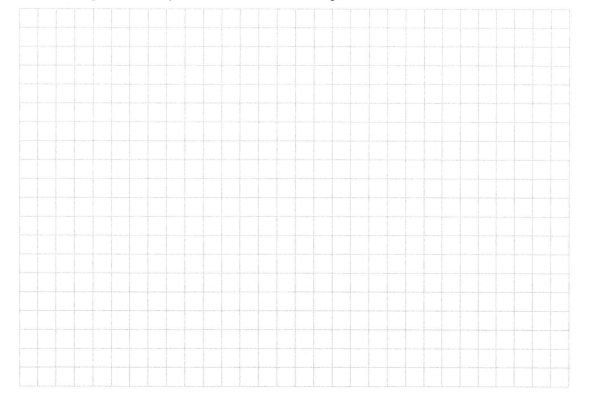

36 Star Polygons

Introduction

If you don't have the program *Logo* on the school network, a free version can be downloaded from www.softronix.com/logo.html and would be very useful for this lesson. In this lesson, learners explore star shapes and calculate the angles needed for different numbers of points. Ideas of interior and exterior angles are useful and extend well to concave polygons from the more familiar setting of convex ones.

Aims and outcomes

- Calculate interior and exterior angles in polygons.
- Contrast the properties of concave and convex polygons.

Lesson starter (10 minutes)

Look at this drawing and describe what you see.

How many different lengths are there? How many different angles?

It is an octagon (8 sides) and it is equilateral, since all the sides are the same length. But it is clearly not equiangular, since there are two sizes of interior angle, one acute and one reflex, so it is not regular. Since it has reflex angles, it is concave.

What symmetry does it have?

It has 4 lines of symmetry and order 4 rotational symmetry.

Can you draw another shape that is similar to this one – from the same 'family'?

Learners might interpret this in various ways. Initially just attempting to copy it accurately with ruler and protractor could be useful. They might try varying the lengths of the sides, making enlarged or reduced versions. Learners may think that all the lengths have to be the same in order to make it join up, but that is not the case:

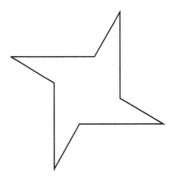

Here, by having two different lengths of line, the order 4 rotational symmetry has been preserved but the lines of symmetry have gone.

Main lesson (30 minutes)

Give out the Task Sheets and encourage learners to examine the stars carefully, perhaps using a protractor and a ruler. If you have access to computers running Logo (available free from www. softronix.com/logo.html), learners can try to draw these and other stars themselves, which is an excellent way of seeing whether they have calculated the correct angles.

Plenary (15 minutes)

All the stars have the same size reflex angles of 240°. The acute angles at each point are different, and their value is what determines the number of points each star has.

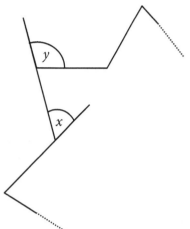

Here is part of a star, with part of an interior reflex angle, x, and an exterior angle at a point, y, marked.

Suppose that the star has n points. Then it will have $2n$ sides and $2n$ vertices, so its total interior angle will be $180(2n - 2) = 360(n - 1)°$. The diagram shows that the interior angle at a point is $180 - y$ and at a reflex angle is $180 + x$. So the total interior angle must also be $n(180 - y + 180 + x) = n(360 + x - y)$.

So $360(n - 1) = n(360 + x - y)$, meaning that $n(y - x) = 360$, so $y = \dfrac{360}{n} + x$. For all the stars on the Task Sheet, x was set equal to 60°, so $y = \dfrac{360}{n} + 60$, and the following lines of code were used to draw them:

n	Number of points	Code
8	4	`repeat 4 [fd 60 lt 60 fd 60 rt 150]`
10	5	`repeat 5 [fd 60 lt 60 fd 60 rt 132]`
12	6	`repeat 6 [fd 60 lt 60 fd 60 rt 120]`
14	7	`repeat 7 [fd 60 lt 60 fd 60 rt 111.4]`
16	8	`repeat 8 [fd 60 lt 60 fd 60 rt 105]`
18	9	`repeat 9 [fd 60 lt 60 fd 60 rt 100]`
20	10	`repeat 10 [fd 60 lt 60 fd 60 rt 96]`

Using code such as `repeat 10 [fd 50 lt 60 fd 10 rt 96]`, learners can generate cogwheel-type drawings such as this:

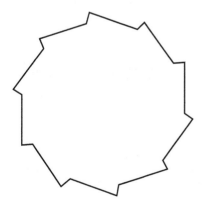

Homework (5 minutes)

Learners could attempt to make any one of these drawings by hand, using ruler and protractor. It is a good idea to use a very large sheet of paper (e.g. A3 size) if you have a shape with many points. The more accurate you are about the angles at the vertices, the more chance it has of looking approximately symmetrical and joining up at the end. It is probably sensible to begin with a shape with a small number of points, but it is more fun not to be sensible!

To make it harder

Confident learners could be asked to predict what this code will draw, and why:

```
repeat 9 [fd 100 rt 160]
```

It will make a star nonagon (star enneagon), with nine points:

Why 160°? What will happen if you vary this angle? What angle do you need to get other star polygons?

For a star *n*-gon, you need $\frac{360m}{n}$, where *m* is positive integer. The variable *m* represents the number of full revolutions, and therefore influences the number of crossings made. The above star enneagon has *n* = 9 and *m* = 3. With *n* = 9 still but *m* = 2, the angle becomes 80° and a simpler star enneagon is produced:

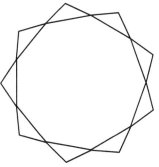

Higher values of *m* and *n* can lead to beaut.ifully intricate star polygons. Learners could try to work out the values of *m* and *n* for a drawing such as this.

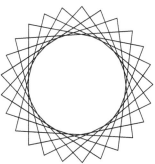

This one has *m* = 7 and *n* = 25. For more information, see De Villiers, M. (1999) 'Stars: A Second Look', *Mathematics in School*, 28, (5), 30.

To make it easier

Learners who find this very difficult could be encouraged to experiment with the software. If some of their attempts don't join up, they could estimate how many more stages are necessary, altering the number following 'repeat' in the code or the sizes of the angles.

Star Polygons

Look at these stars.

What is the same and what is different about them?

Measure or calculate the angles needed to make stars like these.

What patterns do you find?
Can you explain them?

37

Street Race

Introduction
There are some problems in which drawing a diagram really assists. In this lesson, a complicated kinematics problem becomes more accessible when a travel graph is drawn for each person involved. These graphs could be qualitative, illustrating the general idea, or quantitative (on graph paper), showing exactly how many times (and when, and where) the different runners meet.

Aims and outcomes
- Carry out calculations involving speed, distance and time.
- Draw travel graphs to represent and solve a problem.

Lesson starter (10 minutes)
Suppose two people start running in the same direction from the same spot, one at 3 metres per second and one at 4 metres per second but the slower one leaves first. The 4 metres per second runner leaves 10 seconds later. How long does it take him to catch up with the first one? How far have they travelled in this time?

Learners may approach this using informal methods and obtain the correct answer. At a time t seconds after the slow runner leaves, he has travelled a distance of $3t$ metres and (provided that $t > 10$), the second one has travelled $4(t - 10)$ metres. When the second runner catches the first, $3t = 4(t - 10)$, so $3t = 4t - 40$, so $t = 40$ seconds, and the distance travelled is $3 \times 40 = 4 \times 30 = 120$ metres. Learners could also solve this by trial and improvement or by drawing a graph. An easier calculation results from thinking about this in terms of *relative* velocity: When the second runner leaves, the first has already covered $10 \times 3 = 30$ metres. The difference in velocity is 1 metre per second, and the second runner has to cover 30 metres at this relative speed, which will take 30 seconds. So they meet after 40 seconds and a distance of 120 metres, as before.

Main lesson (30 minutes)

Give out the Task Sheets and allow time for learners to make sense of the problem. Providing graph paper might nudge learners in the direction of accurate travel graphs.

Plenary (15 minutes)
What did you decide about Sam and Tony? When did you think they would pass each other? Why?
Learners may find it helpful to draw 'travel graphs' such as the following:

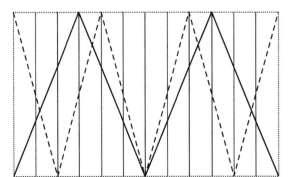

Sam ——————

Tony - - - - -

Resources for Teaching Mathematics: 11–14
TEACHER SHEET

This shows that Sam and Tony meet five times, since this is the number of intersections of the graphs. Learners may conjecture that this is because Sam does two trips and Tony does three trips, and 2 + 3 = 5, and this may encourage them to check other cases. The meetings happen at 1.2 min, 3.6 min, 6 min, 8.4 min and 10.8 min (i.e. every 2.4 minutes).

A simpler situation would be where Tony does four trips in the same time that Sam does two. This time, Sam and Tony meet six times, at 1 min, 3 min, 5 min, 7 min, 9 min and 11 min (i.e. every 2 minutes). On this occasion all the meeting times are integer numbers of minutes.

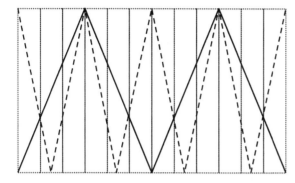

Sam   ———

Tony - - - - -

In general, if Sam does s trips and Tony does t trips, both in 12 minutes, then they will meet at times $\dfrac{6(2n+1)}{s+t}$ minutes, where $n = 0, 1, 2, 3, \ldots, (s+t-1)$. The highest possible value of n will be the largest value for which $\dfrac{6(2n+1)}{s+t} < 12$, so $6(2n+1) < 12(s+t)$, which means that $2n+1 < 2s+2t$, so $n < s+t-\dfrac{1}{2}$. Since n must be an integer, the largest possible value is $(s+t-1)$. Therefore Sam and Tony will meet $(s+t)$ times (since we are counting from $n = 0$ up to, and including, $n = s+t-1$).

One way to see this is to imagine continuing the lines vertically, as shown below.

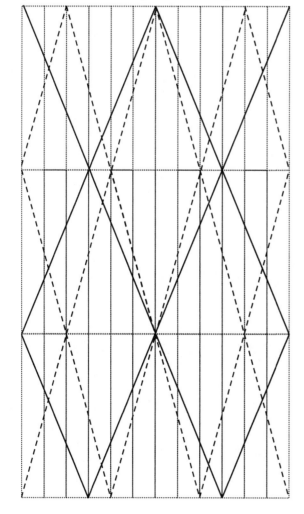

Sam   ———

Tony - - - - -

Meetings happen when the lines $y = \dfrac{sx}{6}$ and $y = -\dfrac{tx}{6} + (2n + 1)$ meet, for values of $n = 0, 1, 2, \ldots$

Solving simultaneously, we obtain $\dfrac{sx}{6} = -\dfrac{tx}{6} + (2n + 1)$, so $\dfrac{x(s + t)}{6} = 2n + 1$, giving $x = \dfrac{6(2n + 1)}{s + t}$ minutes for the range of values of n given above.

Learners are unlikely to approach this in such an abstract way, but may generalize from specific results and justify their patterns with less algebraic arguments. These results are included because they may be helpful for the teacher leading discussion.

Homework (5 minutes)

Learners could find out (or be given) the details of a 'bleep test'. *What speeds does someone have to run at during the various stages? Why?*

To make it harder

Learners confident with this work could explore the situation where Sam and Tony run in a circle.

Sam runs round a circle, doing two complete circuits in 12 minutes. Tony starts at the diametrically opposite point, running the opposite way and doing three complete circuits in 12 minutes. How many times do they cross? And where and when?

Measuring angles between a radius and a diameter through Sam's starting position, in the direction of Sam's motion, at time t, Sam's angle θ_S will be $\theta_S = 60t$ and Tony's angle will be $\theta_T = 180 - 90t$, so these will be equal if $60t = 180 - 90t + 360n$, where n is an integer, so $t = 1.2 + 2.4n$. So the first time when they will meet is when $n = 0$ and $t = 1.2$ minutes. The following meetings happen at 3.6 min, 6 min, 8.4 min and 10.8 min (i.e. every 2.4 minutes), exactly as for the straight street. The problems are equivalent and, in general, if Sam does S circuits in 12 minutes and Tony does T circuits in 12 minutes, then $\theta_S = 30St$ and $\theta_T = 180 - 30Tt$, so $30St = 180 - 30Tt + 360n$, leading to $t = \dfrac{6(2n + 1)}{S + T}$, just as before. We can imagine distorting the circle into an ellipse, with starting points at the sharp ends, and nothing in the problem changes; if we continue squashing the ellipse in this way, we eventually end up with the situation described on the Task Sheet.

To make it easier

Learners who find this hard to envisage could begin with Tony making *two* trips in the same time that Sam makes two trips. This makes the speeds the same as each other and may facilitate drawing the travel graphs:

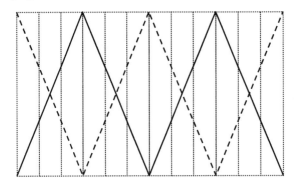

Sam ———

Tony - - - - -

Sam and Tony meet four times, at 1.5 min, 4.5 min, 7.5 min and 10.5 min (i.e. every 3 minutes).

Street Race

© Megan Gay

Sam starts at one end of a street and runs at a steady speed to the other end, and back again, *twice*, arriving back where she started after 12 minutes.

At the same time, Tony starts at the opposite end of the street and runs back and forth *three* times, also at a steady speed, and also finishing back where he started after 12 minutes.

How many times do you think Sam and Tony meet? Why?

Where do you think they meet?
When do you think they meet?

What happens if you change the number of lengths Sam and Tony do?
Sam always starts and finishes at one end and Tony always starts and finishes at the other end.

Try to find situations where all the meetings happen at *integer* numbers of minutes.
When do you think this happens? Why?

38

Symmetrical Possibilities

Introduction

Possibility tables, such as the one used on the Task Sheet for this lesson, give learners the opportunity to generate their own examples, subject to systematically varying constraints along the sides. In this lesson, the constraints involve two different aspects of symmetry in two dimensions: line symmetry and rotational symmetry. Learners will need to engage with the possibility of *impossibility*, since some of the cells in the table cannot be occupied by any shape, and this is one of the possibilities inherent in Possibility tables.

Aims and outcomes

- Understand and use line symmetry in two dimensions.
- Understand and use rotational symmetry in two dimensions.
- Use the properties of different polygons to reason about their symmetry.

Lesson starter (10 minutes)

Look at these mathematical symbols:

$$\% + - \times \div \theta \approx \% \int \Sigma$$
$$\pi \int \Delta \infty > \Rightarrow \cup \therefore \varnothing \neq$$

Write or draw a symbol in this list that has:

- *order 2 rotational symmetry*
- *two lines of symmetry*
- *more than two lines of symmetry*
- *more order of rotational symmetry than number of lines of symmetry.*

Draw a shape with the fewest lines of symmetry.

Draw a shape with the highest order of rotational symmetry.

Learners could answer on mini-whiteboards. The symmetry properties of the symbols are shown in the table below.

Symbol	Number of lines of symmetry	Order of rotational symmetry
$\pi \; \Delta$	0	1
$\neq \approx \% \int$	0	2
$\Sigma \infty > \Rightarrow \cup$	1	1
$- \div \theta \varnothing$	2	2
$\therefore$	3	3
$+ \times$	4	4

So possible answers would be:

Order 2 rotational symmetry: ≠ ≈ % ∫ − ÷ θ ∅

Two lines of symmetry: − ÷ θ ∅

More than two lines of symmetry: ∴ + ×

More order of rotational symmetry than number of lines of symmetry: π Δ ≠ ≈ % ∫

A shape with the fewest lines of symmetry: π Δ

A shape with the highest order of rotational symmetry: + ×

Main lesson (30 minutes)

Give out the Task Sheets (it would be best if you can enlarge them onto A3 when photocopying them). Ask learners to use pencil to sketch, or describe, possible shapes that could go in each of the cells. If they think any cell is impossible, they should say so and try to say why. Learners may think of shapes and then see where they fit in the table, or they might 'aim' for a particular cell. Sometimes a small modification of a shape that will fit in one cell will enable it to go in another. Learners might wish to extend the table for values greater than 6.

Plenary (15 minutes)

Which cells did you fill? Did you think that any cells were impossible? Which ones? Why? Were there any surprises?

Typically, someone will have an example for a cell which someone else thinks is impossible, leading to useful discussion. There may be moments of revelation when they find a shape such as the one below, which has an order of rotational symmetry of 5 but *no lines* of symmetry.

Homework (5 minutes)

The letters of the alphabet (in upper case Arial font) are placed into a bag and one is pulled out at random. What is the probability of choosing a letter with exactly one line of symmetry? What is the probability of choosing a letter with an order of rotational symmetry greater than the number of lines of symmetry? What other questions can you ask?

A two-way table is a convenient way of showing the possible outcomes:

		Order of rotational symmetry		
		1	2	
Number of lines of symmetry	0	FGJKLPQR	NSZ	
	1	ABCDEMTUVWY		
	2		HIX	
				O

The letter 'O' does not fit easily, since it has infinitely many lines of symmetry and an infinite order of rotational symmetry. It also matters how the letter 'K' is written: in Arial font it does not have a line of symmetry, but in some other fonts it could have.

p(exactly one line of symmetry) = p(ABCDEMTUVWY) = $\frac{11}{26}$

p(order of rotational symmetry > number of lines of symmetry) = p(FGJKLPQRNSZ) = $\frac{11}{26}$

The answers are the same!

To make it harder

Keen learners could find out about *group theory* and what this has to do with the symmetry of shapes.

To make it easier

Learners who find this hard could begin with the leading diagonal, where the order of rotational symmetry is equal to the number of lines of symmetry: the regular polygons will fit nicely along here.

Symmetrical Possibilities

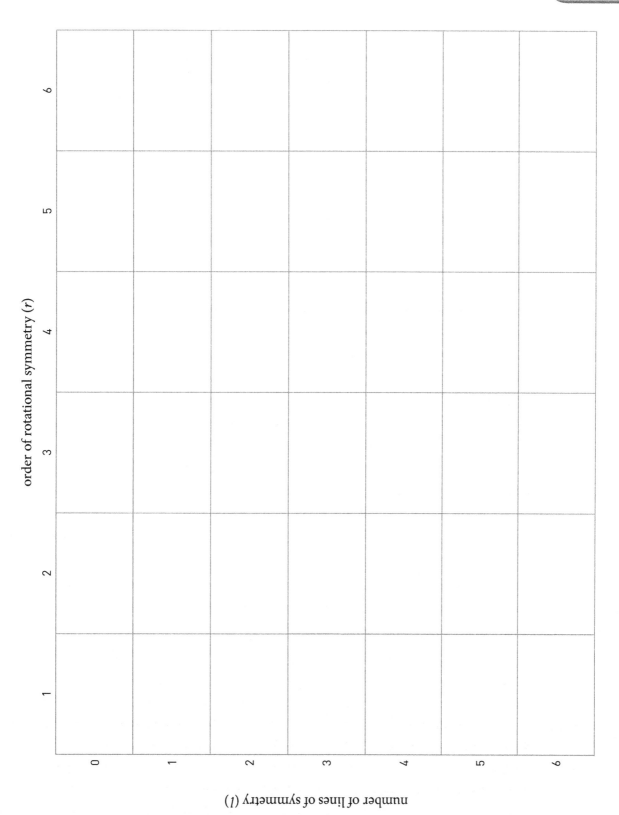

order of rotational symmetry (*r*)

6   5   4   3   2   1

0   1   2   3   4   5   6

number of lines of symmetry (*l*)

39

Take a Breath

Introduction

The physicist Enrico Fermi (1901–1954) was fond of posing estimation/approximation questions, and the idea of using Julius Caesar for the problem given in this lesson appears to have originated with him. There are obvious cross-curricular links here with *Avogadro's number* in chemistry and there may also be a spiritual/cultural dimension when learners appreciate the interdependent nature of life on this planet – the interconnectedness of humanity has the potential to challenge individualist Western assumptions.

Aims and outcomes

- Calculate approximate answers by estimating values.
- Use standard form to express very large or very small numbers.

Lesson starter (10 minutes)

Can you take a deep breath, please, and hold it. Now breathe out. OK, now I'm going to ask you something about that, which I'm not expecting you to be able to answer immediately. Instead, I want you to make a list of all the information that you think you would need to know in order to answer the question. *Here's the question: 'What is the probability that one of the atoms you just breathed out had previously been breathed out by Julius Caesar?'*

See what information learners request.

Do you agree that you need to know that?

Some items might be regarded as irrelevant, easy to estimate or negligible.

Main lesson (30 minutes)

Learners should find the necessary figures on the Task Sheet. If there is anything else that they think they need to know, they should estimate it, in the spirit of approximation problems such as this one.

Plenary (15 minutes)

What answers did you get? How did you work them out?

Air

During Caesar's 56-year lifetime, he would have breathed out about $15 \times 60 \times 24 \times 365 \times 56 = 4.4 \times 10^8$ times. Since each breath contains $\frac{1}{2} \times (2.5 \times 10^{22}) = 1.25 \times 10^{22}$ molecules, this means that throughout his life he would have breathed out about $(4.4 \times 10^8) \times (2.5 \times 10^{22}) = 1.1 \times 10^{31}$ molecules. Since the atmosphere is about $\frac{5 \times 10^{18}}{1.2} \times 1000 = 4.2 \times 10^{21}$ litres, it contains about $(4.2 \times 10^{21}) \times (2.5 \times 10^{22}) = 1.1 \times 10^{44}$ molecules, so the molecules that Caesar has breathed out account for about $\frac{1.1 \times 10^{31}}{1.1 \times 10^{44}} = \frac{1}{10^{13}}$ of all the molecules in the atmosphere. So when we breathe out 1.25×10^{22} molecules (one breath), on average we can expect that $\frac{1}{10^{13}} \times (1.25 \times 10^{22}) \approx 10^9$ (i.e. a billion) of them are from Caesar. In fact, even if we just focus on Caesar's *final dying breath* (i.e. just one of the breaths he breathed out during his lifetime), then those 1.25×10^{22} molecules represent about $\frac{1.25 \times 10^{22}}{1.1 \times 10^{44}} = \frac{1}{88 \times 10^{21}}$ of all the molecules in the atmosphere, which is $\frac{1}{88 \times 10^{21}} \times (1.25 \times 10^{22}) \approx 1$, so it's reasonable to suppose that there might be one molecule from Caesar's *dying* breath in every one of our breaths!

Are Caesar's dates important?

The longer he was alive, the more breathing he did, and the more molecules passed through him. Also, he has to have lived long enough ago for enough mixing to have taken place: this argument wouldn't work with someone who died a few years ago.

We have to assume that the molecules have diffused evenly over the planet and not dissolved in the ocean, for example, or been absorbed by plants, or reacted chemically. We assumed that the density of air is uniform and ignored the composition of air (nitrogen, oxygen, etc.). We also assumed that no one ever breathes the same molecules they have already breathed before, which is rather unlikely!

Water

To estimate the amount of water Julius Caesar might have drunk in his 56 years, we could estimate that he drank 2 litres per day (this includes the water present in foods), so this would come to $56 \times 365 \times 2 = 41\,000$ litres in his whole lifetime. So this will correspond to $41\,000 \times (3 \times 10^{25}) = 1.2 \times 10^{30}$ molecules. Since there are $(3 \times 10^{25}) \times (1.4 \times 10^{21}) = 4 \times 10^{46}$ molecules of water in the global system, Caesar's water molecules are $\dfrac{1.2 \times 10^{30}}{4 \times 10^{46}} = \dfrac{1}{3 \times 10^{16}}$ of the total. Taking a glass of water as $100\,cm^3$, there will be 3×10^{24} molecules in the glass, so we might expect $\dfrac{1}{3 \times 10^{16}} \times (3 \times 10^{24}) = 10^8$ to have passed through Caesar.

The *Titanic*

The iceberg contained about $(5 \times 10^8) \times (3 \times 10^{25}) = 1.5 \times 10^{34}$ molecules, which is $\dfrac{1.5 \times 10^{34}}{4 \times 10^{46}} = \dfrac{1}{3 \times 10^{12}}$ of all the molecules in the global system. So in a glass of water we might expect $\dfrac{1}{3 \times 10^{12}} \times (3 \times 10^{24}) = 10^{12}$ (a trillion) to have come from the iceberg the *Titanic* struck! We have assumed that the iceberg fully melted and that the water molecules have been thoroughly mixed in with the other water molecules in the hydrosphere.

Homework (5 minutes)

Find out which famous person had his very last breath captured in a test tube, which is now displayed in a museum.

It was Thomas Edison (1847–1931), and the test tube is in the Henry Ford Museum, in Michigan.

To make it harder

Can you think how you could avoid *breathing any of Caesar's exhaled air or drinking any of the Titanic's iceberg?* You could breathe a chemically synthesized oxygen/nitrogen mixture or drink water from an iceberg that dated from the ice age, long before the *Titanic* hit the iceberg!

To make it easier

Learners who find this particularly hard could begin by estimating the number of molecules in the air in the classroom.

Take a Breath

Julius Caesar (100 BCE – 44 BCE)

Density of air = 1.2 kg/m^3

Mass of earth's atmosphere = 5×10^{18} kg

Volume of air breathed out in one normal breath (tidal volume) = 500 cm^3

Average number of breaths per minute = 15

Number of molecules in 1 litre of air = 2.5×10^{22}

Air

How likely do you think it is that one or more of the molecules in one of your breaths was also breathed out by Julius Caesar in one of his breaths? Why?

Do some calculations to test this out.

Water

Suppose you take a drink of water. How likely do you think it is that some of those molecules were drunk by Julius Caesar? Why?

Do some calculations to test this out.

Density of water = 1 kg/litre

Total mass of water on earth = 1.4×10^{21} kg

Number of molecules in 1 kg of water = 3×10^{25}

The *Titanic*'s iceberg

What about the iceberg that sank the ship *Titanic* in 1912? Do you think it is likely that you have drunk some of the water molecules from that iceberg? Why/why not?

Do some calculations to test this out.

Estimated mass of iceberg = 5×10^{8} kg

What sort of assumptions do you think are necessary for these calculations?

How valid do you think they are? Why?

40

The Playground Problem

Introduction

This question is normally known as the 'art gallery problem'; in this lesson a different spin is put on it, involving teachers patrolling in a school playground. The problem sounds straightforward and is applicable to real-life situations, such as surveillance of museums. Although the solution is quite simple to state, a proof involves considerable thought.

Aims and outcomes

- Examine the properties of polygons.
- Solve a practical minimizing problem.
- Use strategic thinking to place objects in optimal places.

Lesson starter (10 minutes)

Do you think that CCTV cameras are a good thing or not? Why?

Learners are likely to contrast ideas of safety with those of liberty, even though they are unlikely to use this language. They may question the motives behind the 'surveillance state' or they may wish for more. They might refer to recent films that they have seen on related themes.

Do you think we should have CCTV cameras in school? Why/why not? (You could ask this question regardless of the extent to which you have them in your school.)

One study (www.urbaneye.net/results/ue_wp6.pdf) has estimated that there are about 4 285 000 CCTV cameras in the UK, or about one camera for every 14 people.

How many do you think we would need to cover this classroom, or the dining hall, etc.?

Learners may comment on the shape and size of the room as important factors or question the purpose for which you are watching the room.

Main lesson (30 minutes)

Give out the Task Sheets and encourage learners to think carefully about every nook and cranny.

Plenary (15 minutes)

One possible solution uses nine teachers, but there are many other possibilities:

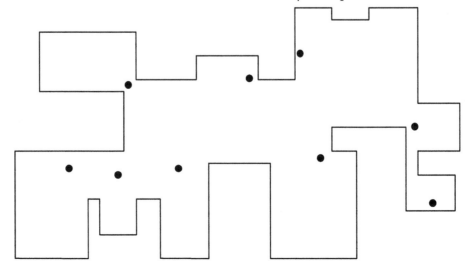

We assume that the teachers are stationary, that each one can see 360° about their point and as far into the distance as necessary.

One approach is to 'triangulate' (split into triangles), since every n-gon can be dissected into $(n - 2)$ triangles, and one teacher can cover each, so you are never going to need more than $(n - 2)$ teachers. However, this is not a very low upper bound.

If a rectilinear polygon (a closed polygon with only horizontal and vertical edges) has n edges, then you will never need more than $\left\lfloor \dfrac{n}{4} \right\rfloor$ teachers, where the brackets indicate the 'floor' function, the greatest integer less than or equal to the value (i.e. 'rounding down to the next lowest integer'). For example, a rectangle, with $n = 4$, needs only one teacher, who can be anywhere in the interior.

Any convex polygon can be covered by just one teacher, who can be anywhere in the interior. For other n-gons, a maximum of $\left\lfloor \dfrac{n}{3} \right\rfloor$ may be needed. No 'pillars' or 'holes' are permitted.

What are the hardest shaped rooms to do? Which ones use up the most teachers for the fewest extra sides?

Shapes like the one below are teacher-intensive – not a good design for a playground if teachers want to enjoy their coffee breaks!

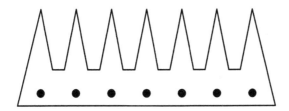

With $n = 21$, the diagram shows that seven teachers are needed. No 21-gon will ever need more than this.

(Interestingly, in the three-dimensional version of the problem, even placing a teacher at every vertex of a polyhedron may not be enough.) For a nice summary of this problem, see Picker, S. H. (2007) 'Chvátal's art gallery theorem!', *Mathematics in School*, 36, (3), 2–3.

Homework (5 minutes)

Look at some museum plans on the internet. Are the layouts of the rooms well designed from the point of view of minimizing the number of guards necessary? What other factors influence museum layouts?

Some museums are housed in historic buildings, where there may be severe limitations on possible layouts. Also, if you had one huge rectangle, could it really be covered adequately by just one guard?

In this problem, we supposed that teachers can monitor 360° about their position. (Everyone knows that teachers have eyes in the backs of their heads!) Find out about field of view *and how it varies for different animals.*

Human beings can see almost 180° horizontally (and 100° vertically) without turning their heads, although they can see fine detail only in a relatively small cone straight ahead. Predators, such as humans, tend to have eyes at the front of the head, giving the advantage of binocular vision but a lower field of view, whereas animals that are predominantly preyed upon tend to have eyes on either side of their heads and a much wider field of view, so they can see when something is coming.

To make it harder

Keen students could examine the *fortress problem*, which is the opposite situation, where you are guarding the whole *exterior* of a polygon. (Here the assumption that the guards can see as far as necessary is rather strained, like their eyes!) For a convex n-gon, $\frac{n}{2}$ is always sufficient if n is even, since you can place a guard at every other vertex. If n is odd, you need $\frac{n+1}{2}$, so this can be summed up by saying that $\left\lceil \frac{n}{2} \right\rceil$ is always sufficient, where the brackets indicate the 'ceiling' function, the lowest integer greater than or equal to the value ('rounding up to the next integer'). In fact, fewer guards are needed if they do not have to be on the edge of the polygon – if they can be anywhere in the exterior region then $\left\lceil \frac{n}{3} \right\rceil$ is always sufficient.

To make it easier

Beginning with a rectangle and modifying it in simple ways may be a good way for learners to get into the task and see what is possible.

The Playground Problem

Here is a plan drawing of a rather complicated school playground.

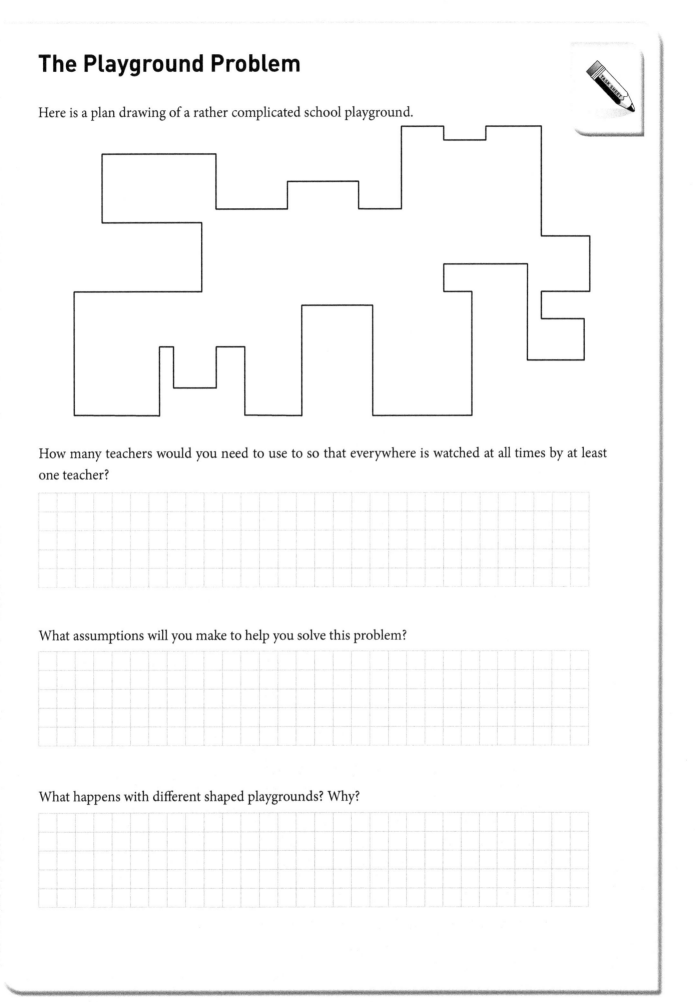

How many teachers would you need to use to so that everywhere is watched at all times by at least one teacher?

What assumptions will you make to help you solve this problem?

What happens with different shaped playgrounds? Why?

41

The Tailor's Rule of Thumb

Introduction

Sometimes one simple measurement can give a lot of information about something much more complicated. For example, in first aid, taking someone's pulse or temperature can be very informative and give clues about a wide range of possible conditions. In this lesson, thumb circumference is used to predict various body measurements. This idea comes from *Gulliver's Travels* (Jonathan Swift, 1726):

> Then they measured my right thumb, and desired no more; for by a mathematical computation, that twice round the thumb is once round the wrist, and so on to the neck and the waist, . . . they fitted me exactly.

Though from fiction, this idea is actually used in schools in some parts of the world to size a large number of pupils very quickly for their uniforms. There are obvious cross-curricular links with body proportions in both art and biology. It will be important in this lesson to make sure that pupils are not made to feel self-conscious about their own proportions – the starter may help with this, emphasizing that 'normality' covers a very wide range and that different proportions may have advantages and disadvantages in different situations.

Aims and outcomes

- Devise ways of testing statistical hypotheses.
- Examine connections between human proportions.
- Use ratio to describe relationships.

Lesson starter (10 minutes)

A person's *ape index* is the ratio of their arm span (finger tip to finger tip) to their height. *Stand near a wall and touch the tip of the fingers of one hand on the floor and stretch up the wall with the other hand as far as you can reach. Keep your finger at that point and stand up straight. Is the top of your head above or below that mark?*

An ape index greater than 1 is thought to be an advantage in rock climbing and swimming but an ape index less than 1 is an advantage in weightlifting.

What other body proportions do you think might be important in sports? Why? Do you think you can guess at a sportsperson's sport just by looking at their physique? Why/why not?

Main lesson (30 minutes)

Here are some claims about human body proportions:

$$\text{Elbow to finger} = \frac{1}{4} \text{ of height}$$

$$\text{Length of foot} = \frac{1}{6} \text{ of height}$$

$$\text{Top to bottom of head} = \frac{1}{8} \text{ of height}$$

$$\text{Length of hand} = \frac{1}{10} \text{ of height}$$

$$\text{Eyes to chin} = \frac{1}{2} \text{ of head height}$$

Do you believe them? How accurate do you think they are? How would you check to see?

Encourage learners to be specific, stating how many people they would measure, how they would choose them, where exactly they would measure from and to, and what they would do with all the numbers they obtained.

Give out the Task Sheets and encourage learners to plan their experiment.

Plenary (15 minutes)

Different learners will have developed different plans. It is unlikely that they will be able to find all the necessary data on the internet, so they will need to decide how to collect their own. This could either be done in school or as a homework.

Exactly what data will you collect? What will you measure? How many people?

How will you collect it? From whom? Does it matter if they are adults or children? Where and when will you do it?

What calculations will you do? What graphs will you draw?

Different learners (or groups of learners) could test different hypotheses. One option for processing the data would be to plot a scatter graph of the measured values against the predicted ones and look for correlation.

There are interesting studies on how people perceive body proportions; for example, Bianchi, I., Savardi, U. and Bertamini, M. (2008) 'Estimation and Representation of Head Size' [people overestimate the size of their head – evidence starting from the fifteenth century], *British Journal of Psychology*, 99, 513–31, available at www.liv.ac.uk/vp/Publications/Bianchi2008.pdf

Homework (5 minutes)

Learners could gather their data for homework. Alternatively, they could find out about the *Vitruvian Man*. This is a drawing by Leonardo da Vinci, showing the 'ideal' proportions of a human being. *Which proportions does it show?*

Find out how body-mass index works. Can you use it on teenagers?

Learners who still possess dolls (or who are willing to admit to doing so!) could measure the body proportions of their favourite dolls and scale up to life-size to see how realistic (or not) they are. Some well-known brands of doll have legs so thin that they would be likely to snap if they tried to run!

To make it harder

Confident learners could consider this: *Which is larger when you buy trousers – waist measurement or inside leg? For most people, it is the waist measurement. Look at some cylindrical objects and try to decide 'by eye' which is larger – the circumference or the height?*

It can be interesting to try this with different-shaped glasses and then check with a tape measure or a piece of string. It can be quite deceptive, because it is nearly always further around the top, even with a champagne glass. Not many things we drink out of have a greater height than circumference; two notable exceptions are a bottle and a straw!

Make a cylinder for which these two distances are the same. Does it look how you expected it to look?

You can easily do this by starting with a square of paper and bending it round until one edge meets the parallel edge.

To make it easier

All learners should be able to develop some ideas about how they would establish whether one of these claims is true or not.

The Tailor's Rule of Thumb

Some people don't like having to try on clothes in a shop. They also don't like having lots of measurements taken when they want to buy something.

A tailor could just measure around a customer's thumb and then use this method to find the right size for a shirt or trousers.

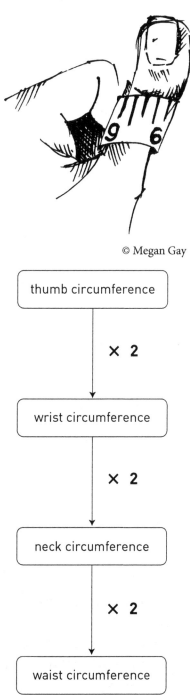

© Megan Gay

thumb circumference

× 2

wrist circumference

× 2

neck circumference

× 2

waist circumference

How well do you think this works? Why?

42

The Totient Function

Introduction

The *Euler totient function* $\varphi(n)$ of a positive integer n is the number of positive integers less than n that are co-prime to n (i.e. that have no common factors with n other than 1). For example, $\varphi(6) = 2$, since from the integers 1 to 6 only 1 and 5 are co-prime to 6. This lesson utilizes this idea for a task involving reducible fractions (i.e. ones that cancel down). Learners investigate how many fractions between 0 and 1, with a given denominator n, cancel down. For $n > 1$, this will be equal to $n - \varphi(n) - 1$. You might want to use the word 'reducible' with learners, or stick to the more familiar terms relating to 'cancelling down'.

Aims and outcomes

- Explore patterns in reducible fractions.
- Understand and use equivalent fractions.

Lesson starter (10 minutes)

How many different proper fractions are there with a 9 in the denominator? Why?

(We are taking 'fraction' to mean $\frac{\text{positive integer}}{\text{positive integer}}$, and '9 in the denominator' to mean 'exactly 9'; not '39', for example. A *proper* fraction has a numerator smaller than the denominator.)

There are eight possible proper fractions: $\frac{1}{9}, \frac{2}{9}, \frac{3}{9}, \frac{4}{9}, \frac{5}{9}, \frac{6}{9}, \frac{7}{9}, \frac{8}{9}$.

Why are there eight?

There will always be one fewer than the denominator number, because $\frac{9}{9}$ would not be a *proper* fraction. So, for a denominator of n there will be $(n - 1)$ proper fractions.

Which ones cancel down? Why?

Only $\frac{3}{9}$ and $\frac{6}{9}$ cancel down, because the numerator and denominator have a common factor greater than 1 (3, in this case).

Main lesson (30 minutes)

Give out the Task Sheets and encourage learners to experiment with different sizes of denominator and write down what they notice.

Plenary (15 minutes)

What did you discover? Did you find any denominators that led to no *cancelling down?*

Which denominators created the most *cancelling down? Why do you think that was?*

The table on the next page shows the number of fractions that cancel down for different denominators, n. (For example, the shaded cell shows that with a denominator of 24 (coming from 20 + 4), there are 15 fractions that cancel down.)

Even denominators (with the exception of 2) lead to odd numbers of reducible fractions, and odd denominators lead to even numbers of reducible fractions, so the numbers in the table are alternately odd and even. The zeroes come on the *prime* denominators, because if n is prime (and greater than 2) then none of the numbers from 2 to $(n - 1)$ can be factors of it. If you want a denominator that creates lots of cancelling down, then having a large number of factors helps, but the size of the number is also important, since all of the answers must be smaller than n.

	0	1	2	3	4	5	6	7	8	9
0			0	0	1	0	3	0	3	2
10	5	0	7	0	7	6	7	0	11	0
20	11	8	11	0	15	4	13	8	15	0
30	21	0	15	12	17	10	23	0	19	14
40	23	0	29	0	23	20	23	0	31	6
50	29	18	27	0	35	14	31	20	29	0
60	43	0	31	26	31	16	45	0	35	24
70	45	0	47	0	37	34	39	16	53	0
80	47	26	41	0	59	20	43	30	47	0
90	65	18	47	32	47	22	63	0	55	38

The smallest denominator with exactly *four* fractions that cancel down is 25, since $\frac{5}{25}, \frac{10}{25}, \frac{15}{25}$ and $\frac{20}{25}$ are the only ones that cancel down; for five it is 10, since only $\frac{2}{10}, \frac{4}{10}, \frac{5}{10}, \frac{6}{10}$ and $\frac{8}{10}$ cancel down. The table below shows denominators that lead to given numbers of reducible fractions.

Number of fractions between 0 and 1 that cancel down	Possible denominators (<50)
0	Prime numbers
1	4
2	9
3	6, 8
4	25
5	10
6	15, 49
7	12, 14, 16
8	21, 27
9	None
10	35
11	18, 20, 22
12	33

Homework (5 minutes)

Work out the number of reducible tenths, hundredths, thousandths, etc. Is there a pattern here? Why? What happens with a sequence of denominators which are powers of something other than 10? Why?

After tenths, there will be far too many for learners to count individually, so some generalized thinking will be needed. For 100, all even numerators ($\frac{2}{100}, \frac{4}{100}, \frac{6}{100} \ldots$) will lead to reducible fractions, and there are 49 of those (not 50, since we are not including $\frac{100}{100}$). On top of this will be numerators 5, 15, 25, ... and there will be 10 of these, giving a total of 59 reducible fractions. Similar thinking leads to the following results:

Denominator	Number of reducible fractions between 0 and 1
10	5
100	49 + 10 = 59
1000	499 + 100 = 599
10 000	4999 + 1000 = 5999

With a denominator of 10^m, we have $\frac{1}{2}(10)^m + 10^{m-1} - 1$ reducible fractions. Other denominators that are powers of a fixed base number also have interesting patterns; for example, with a denominator of 2^m we have $2^{m-1} - 1$ reducible fractions, as shown in the table below.

Denominator	Number of reducible fractions between 0 and 1
2	0
4	1
8	3
16	7
32	15
64	31

To make it harder

Confident learners could explore what happens with fractions *greater than 1*.

Are there the same number of reducible fractions between 1 and 2 as there are between 0 and 1? Does it matter whether you write them as 'top-heavy' fractions or as mixed numbers?

Yes, there is the same number of reducible fractions between any two consecutive integers. It doesn't make any difference how these fractions are written, because the mixed number '$a\frac{b}{n}$', where a, b and n are integers and $b < n$, is equal to $\frac{an + b}{n}$, and $(an + b)$ will be a multiple of n exactly when b is a multiple of n, since an is necessarily a multiple of n.

To make it easier

Learners who find this difficult could be encouraged (or helped) to record their results in an orderly way. Listing the factors of the denominator may help learners to spot which fractions cancel down, if that is the difficulty.

The Totient Function

There are seven fractions between 0 and 1 that have a denominator of 8.

$$\frac{1}{8}, \frac{2}{8}, \frac{3}{8}, \frac{4}{8}, \frac{5}{8}, \frac{6}{8}, \frac{7}{8}$$

Which ones cancel down? Why?

How many fractions are there between 0 and 1 that have a denominator of 7?
How many of them will cancel down? Why?

Look at different denominators and find out how many fractions cancel down each time.

Can you find a denominator with *exactly four* fractions that cancel down?
Can you find one with *exactly five* fractions that cancel down?

Find out as much as you can about how many fractions with a certain denominator cancel down.

43

Three Consecutive Numbers

Introduction

Numerical magic tricks of the 'think of a number' variety are often presented and analysed in mathematics lessons and tend to generate 'Why does it work?' questions from learners. In this lesson, learners choose their own operations and explore what happens with different starting numbers, leading to conjectures which can be proved algebraically. Confident learners might begin by analyzing the processes algebraically; alternatively, specializing with particular numbers initially helps to get a sense of what is happening, and perhaps some ideas why.

Aims and outcomes

- Draw conclusions from algebraic expressions.
- Factorize linear expressions.
- Simplify algebraic expressions.

Lesson starter (15 minutes)

Consecutive numbers are integers that go up in ones. Can someone give us three consecutive numbers, please.

If learners give very large numbers, or negative ones, it doesn't matter – you can accept whatever is offered. Write them on the board.

We're going to multiply the first one by 3, the second one by 4 and the third one by 5.

What do you notice about the answer?

Learners may notice many things, such as that the answer is a large integer – with enough examples, someone may notice that it is 12 lots of the middle number plus 2. Someone may comment that the number is always even. It is fine if learners spot other things.

One way to analyse this is to say that in a sense there are only two different sets of consecutive numbers: {even, odd, even} and {odd, even, odd}. So, we are producing either $3 \times$ even $+ 4 \times$ odd $+ 5 \times$ even, which will be even + even + even = even, or $3 \times$ odd $+ 4 \times$ even $+ 5 \times$ odd = odd + even + odd = even. Either way the answer will be even. Using algebra, if the three consecutive numbers are $(x - 1)$, x and $(x + 1)$, then our number is $3(x - 1) + 4x + 5(x + 1) = 12x + 2 = 2(6x + 1)$. (Learners might be happier using x, $(x + 1)$ and $(x + 2)$ as the three consecutive numbers.)

Main lesson (25 minutes)

Give out the Task Sheets and encourage learners to have a go with different starting numbers. Some may try to use algebra straight away to analyse the problem. You might choose to encourage 'generalizers' to do a bit more specializing and 'specializers' to do some generalizing – or you might leave individual learners to decide for themselves. If very different kinds of activity are going on, it could be useful to stop everyone at some point and have a mini-plenary in which some learners say a little about what they have been doing, in case this gives ideas for others to use.

Plenary (15 minutes)

What did you find out? What things did you try? Did you find any interesting patterns?

Resources for Teaching Mathematics: 11–14
TEACHER SHEET

With the multipliers (2, 4, 10), as given in the flow diagram, we obtain $2(x - 1) + 4x + 10(x + 1)$ $= 16x + 8 = 8(2x + 1)$, so all answers will be an odd multiple of 8. In general, if the three multipliers, in order, are a, b and c, such that $a < b < c$, and all three are integers, then the final value will be $a(x - 1) + bx + c(x + 1) = (a + b + c)x + (c - a)$, so this will be a multiple of $(c - a)$ if $(a + b + c)$ is a multiple of $(c - a)$. In general, the values produced will be multiples of the highest common factor of $(a + b + c)$ and $(c - a)$. So if $(a, b, c) = (2, 5, 8)$ then the values produced will be multiples of HCF(15, 6) = 3, since the algebra will give $15x + 6 = 3(5x + 2)$.

Homework (5 minutes)

Learners could be invited to try to work out how to turn this process into a 'trick' by choosing numbers that will lead to a multiple of 9 every time. For example, if $(a, b, c) = (2, 5, 11)$ then the final answer will always be a multiple of 9, so by calling for repeated digit sums on the final answer, this will always lead to 9 in the end, which could be an impressive trick. So if your chosen consecutive numbers happened to be 53, 54 and 55, you would calculate $(2 \times 53) + (5 \times 54) + (11 \times 55) = 981$. Adding the digits of 981 gives 18, and adding these digits gives 9. Learners are likely to be able to do this only if they are familiar with the use of divisibility properties and digit sums to create mathematical magic.

To make it harder

Confident learners could try to choose a suitable set of three numbers so that the answers come out to any desired multiple; e.g. choose a set of three multipliers so that whatever set of three consecutive integers are used you end up with a final answer that is a multiple of 7, say. To get a multiple of 7, for instance, you could use the multipliers 2, 3 and 9. The table below shows various multiples and possible triples that will work.

Multiple	Possible triple
2	3, 4, 5
3	2, 2, 5
4	2, 4, 6
5	2, 6, 7
6	1, 4, 7
7	2, 3, 9
8	2, 4, 10 (given)

To make it easier

Learners who find this hard could use a calculator and perhaps write down the separate stages, so as to keep track of the calculations. Those who are getting stuck could be encouraged (or helped) to record their results in a table as they go, to make it easier to see emerging patterns.

Three Consecutive Numbers

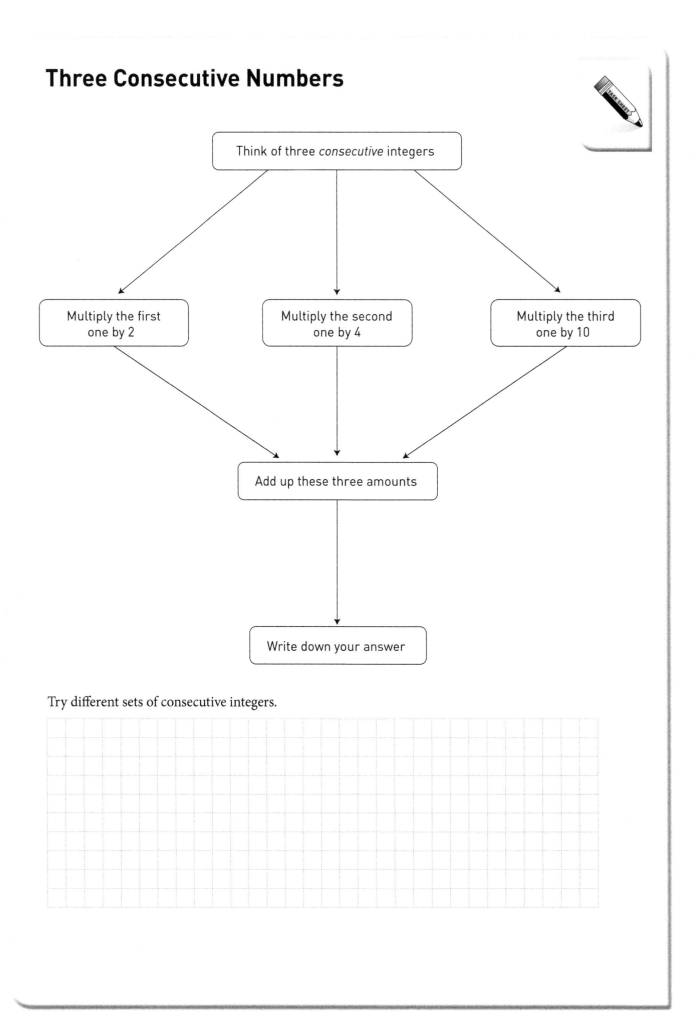

Think of three *consecutive* integers

Multiply the first one by 2

Multiply the second one by 4

Multiply the third one by 10

Add up these three amounts

Write down your answer

Try different sets of consecutive integers.

What stays the same and what changes in your final answer? Can you explain why?

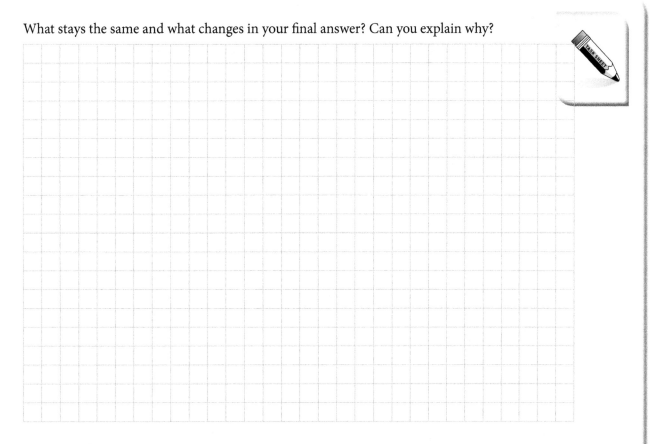

Now try changing the '2', the '4' and the '10' into other integers.
What effect does this have? Can you explain what you find?

44

Transforming Graphs

Introduction

This lesson explores *affine transformations*, which are combinations of linear transformations (reflections, rotations and enlargements) and translations. Translations are different from the linear transformations because they do not (other than the identity translation, $\begin{pmatrix} 0 \\ 0 \end{pmatrix}$) map the origin to itself – thus, they cannot be represented by 2×2 matrices in the way that the linear transformations can. Learners will explore the effects of these transformations on straight-line graphs; this complements the more common work of transforming geometrical shapes. In each case, a straight line is produced and learners can find the equations of these lines and try to generalize their results.

Aims and outcomes

- Carry out linear transformations and translations and investigate the results.
- Draw and identify straight-line graphs.

Lesson starter (15 minutes)

Show the graph $y = 2x + 3$ on the board (this could be a sketch or an accurate representation from graph-drawing software).

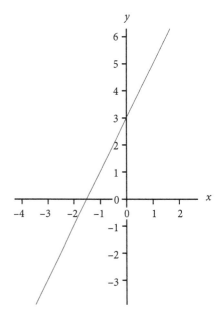

How would you describe this graph?

The words 'gradient' and 'intercept' may be helpful to introduce if learners don't use them.

Describe how it would be if it were reflected in the y-axis.

Learners might comment on the slope or the x-intercept and y-intercept.

What would the equation become?

It would become $y = -2x + 3$. (The 'x' in the equation becomes '$-x$'.)

Describe how it would be if it were reflected in the x-axis.

It would become $y = -2x - 3$. (Effectively, the 'y' in the equation becomes '$-y$'.)

Describe how it would be if it were reflected in the y-axis and then reflected in the x-axis.

Describe how it would be if it were reflected in the x-*axis and then* reflected in the y-*axis.*

Either way round, it would become $y = 2x - 3$. Overall, as far as the line is concerned, these two reflections are equivalent to a translation $\begin{pmatrix} 0 \\ -6 \end{pmatrix}$ or a rotation 180° about the origin. (We are thinking about the line as a whole, rather than where each individual point goes to.)

Main lesson (25 minutes)

Give out the Task Sheets and encourage learners to test their conjectures by drawing or sketching. You might wish to use computers to do the work of drawing the straight-line graphs, or just for checking, if you want the learners to practise sketching them for themselves.

Plenary (15 minutes)

What did you find out? Were you able to find equations for the transformed lines?

General results are given in the table below for the convenience of the teacher, although it is probably more likely, initially at least, that learners will have worked with specific values for m and c.

Transformation of $y = mx + c$	Result
Reflection in y-axis	$y = -mx + c$
Reflection in x-axis	$y = -mx - c$
Reflection in $x = k$	$y = -mx + 2mk + c$
Reflection in $y = k$	$y = -mx + 2k - c$
Translation $\begin{pmatrix} a \\ b \end{pmatrix}$	$y = mx + ma - b + c$ (Note that if the translation is *parallel* to the line, then $\frac{b}{a} = m$, so $ma = b$, giving $y = mx + c$, the original line.)
Rotation 180° about the origin	$y = mx - c$
Rotation 90° clockwise about the origin	$y = \frac{c - x}{m}$, $m \neq 0$ (lines $y = c$ become $x = c$)
Rotation 90° anticlockwise about the origin	$y = \frac{-c - x}{m}$, $m \neq 0$ (lines $y = c$ become $x = -c$)
Rotation 180° about the point (a, b)	$y = mx + 2(b - ma) - c$ (Note that if the point (a, b) lies *on* the line $y = mx + c$, then $b = ma + c$, giving $y = mx + c$, the original line. If $a = b = 0$, we obtain $y = mx - c$, as above.)

Homework (5 minutes)

Learners could be asked to choose one of their results and produce a summary of it, with explanation, perhaps as a poster for the classroom.

To make it harder

Confident learners could explore combinations of transformations. *Does the order matter? When? Why?*

They could also explore transformations of *curves*, such as the parabola $y = x^2$. *Which of the results we found work the same way and which behave differently? Why?*

To make it easier

Learners who find this hard could begin with the line $y = x$ and consider what transformations will leave it unchanged. For example, a translation $\begin{pmatrix} 4 \\ 4 \end{pmatrix}$ or a rotation about $(3, 3)$ by 180° or a reflection in the line $y = -x + 7$, for instance. There are many opportunities here for generalization.

Transforming Graphs

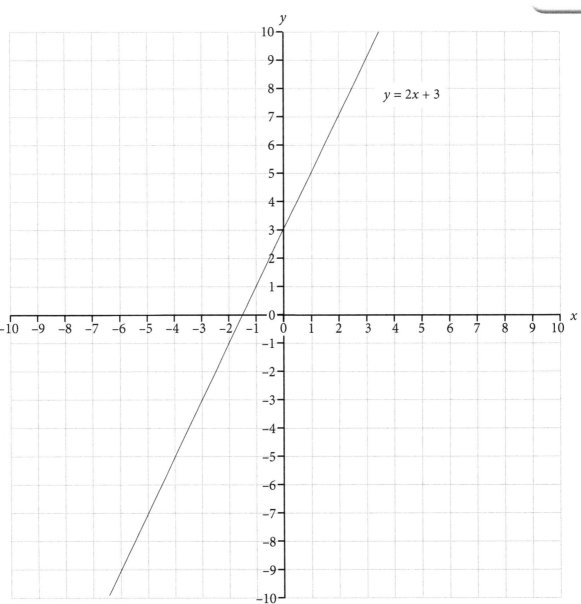

$y = 2x + 3$

What happens to the graph $y = 2x + 3$ if you:

reflect it

in the y-axis?

in the x-axis?

in the y-axis and then in the x-axis?

in the x-axis and then in the y-axis?

in the line $x = 6$?

in the line $y = 2$?

etc.

translate it

$\begin{pmatrix} 1 \\ 2 \end{pmatrix}$?

$\begin{pmatrix} 2 \\ 3 \end{pmatrix}$?

etc.

rotate it

$180°$ about the origin?

$90°$ clockwise about the origin?

$90°$ anticlockwise about the origin?

$180°$ about the point $(3, 4)$?

etc.

Try to find the equations of the lines produced.

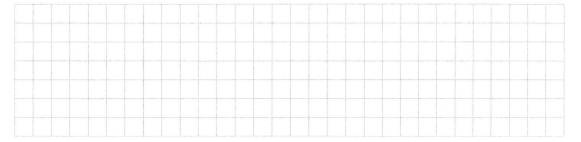

Try to generalize.

What other questions can you ask?

45

Transport Problems

Introduction

In this lesson we consider some classic 'transport problems', which traditionally come in a number of politically incorrect versions, involving cannibals and jealous husbands (not in the same version!). Logical puzzles sometimes provoke the question: 'Is this maths?' Besides the counting of the number of trips and the time, these problems involve the imposition of arbitrary (ludicrous, even) conditions which impose constraints on what is possible. Handling constraints and looking for optimal solutions are highly mathematical processes. Lessons based on these puzzles are likely to be a lot of fun and can appeal to learners who do not often enjoy more traditional mathematics lessons. For more details of problems like this, see Pressman, I. and Singmaster, D. (1989) '"The Jealous Husbands" and "The Missionaries and Cannibals"', *The Mathematical Gazette*, 73, (464), 73–81.

Aims and outcomes

- Develop numeracy skills in a problem-solving context.
- Use logical thinking to find optimal solutions to problems involving constraints.

Lesson starter (15 minutes)

You might have seen this before, but don't worry if you have – we can change it a bit. It starts with a farmer who goes to market and buys a wolf, a goat and a cabbage. He's taking them home and has to cross a river. The boat can only carry him and one other item, so he is going to have to make more than one trip. If he leaves the goat with the cabbage, the goat will eat the cabbage. If he leaves the wolf with the goat, the wolf will eat the goat. How can he get everything safely across the river?

You could choose learners to represent the farmer, the wolf and the goat, perhaps graciously being the cabbage yourself?! (Badges saying who is what might avoid confusion; dressing up would be possible if you are very keen!)

The farmer has to leave the wolf with the cabbage (leaving either other pair will lead to something eating something) and take the goat across to the other end. Then he returns, but whichever thing he takes with him on the second trip will not be compatible with the goat on the other side when he leaves them together to fetch the third item. The trick is to bring back the goat on his second return trip, to prevent any conflicts.

1. The farmer takes the goat to the other side and returns. (The wolf and the cabbage are safe together.)
2. The farmer takes the wolf (or the cabbage) to the other side and returns with the goat.
3. The farmer leaves the goat on the first side and takes the cabbage (or the wolf) over to the other side. (The wolf and the cabbage are safe together on the other side.)
4. The farmer returns and then brings the goat across for the second time.

So, it can be done in 7 trips.

Do you think you can do it in fewer trips?

No. This is the minimum possible.

Main lesson (25 minutes)

Give out the Task Sheets and encourage learners to think about the two transport puzzles presented, perhaps using coloured counters to represent the different people. You might wish to encourage learners to devise a convenient and efficient method of recording their moves, otherwise 'I solved it but I don't remember how!' will be a repeated cry.

Plenary (15 minutes)

Did you think they were possible or impossible? Why? How did you get on? What was your solution? Does anyone have a different solution?

School Trip

This can be solved in the following way (T = teacher; P = pupil):

1. T + P cross
2. T returns
3. 2P cross
4. P returns
5. 2T cross
6. T + P return
7. 2T cross
8. P returns
9. 2P cross.

It cannot be completed in fewer than 9 trips.

Torch and Bridge

This can be done in a minimum of 15 minutes. Learners often start by imagining that A (as the quickest person) would be the best person to ferry everyone else across one by one, but this takes $(2 + 5 + 8) + 2 \times 1 = 17$ minutes, the 2×1 corresponding to the two return trips necessary, of 1 minute each, to bring back the torch. However, it is actually quicker to send the two *slowest* people across together:

1. A and B go across
2. A brings the torch back
3. C and D go across
4. B brings the torch back
5. A and B go across (again).

This takes a total of $2 + 1 + 8 + 2 + 2 = 15$ minutes, and is the quickest possible.

If we let the times needed by A, B, C and D be a, b, c and d respectively (where we will assume that $0 < a < b < c < d$), then the first attempt corresponds to a total time of $2a + b + c + d$, whereas the second one is $a + 3b + d$, so the first method will be longer than the second if and only if $a + c > 2b$, as is the case here, since $1 + 5 > 2 \times 2$. This suggests possible ways to vary the puzzle while retaining this tricky feature. Interestingly, simply increasing d (and leaving the other numbers unchanged) does not affect the optimal strategy. With $(a, b, c, d) = (1, 2, 5, 100)$, the second method is still the best possible, this time taking 107 minutes. For more information, see Rote, G., 'Crossing the Bridge at Night', http://citeseerx.ist.psu.edu/viewdoc/download?doi=10.1.1.6.8855& rep=rep1&type=pdf.

Homework (5 minutes)

This is not easy, but can you devise a transport problem of your own? It could be similar to the ones we have looked at or quite different. Make sure that its solution is not obvious. The trickiest type of puzzle is one in which there is a solution which looks *best but in fact can be beaten with a bit more thought!*

Any particularly good puzzles could perhaps be published in the school magazine or on the school website.

To make it harder

There is likely to be plenty here to occupy all learners, especially if they try to consider within what limits the problems can be varied without destroying their essential features. Interested learners could find out on the internet about other *transport problems.*

To make it easier

Learners who find this hard might benefit from using counters to represent the people and recording each stage (or having someone else do that) as they go. They can be encouraged that everyone finds these puzzles hard and that they have been preserved through the years because they make people scratch their heads!

Transport Problems

School Trip

There are three teachers and three pupils on one side of a river. They have a boat but it can carry only two people. The rule is that at no time can you have more pupils than teachers on either bank (otherwise the teachers would not be safe).

© Megan Gay

- How can you get everybody across?
- What is the smallest number of trips possible? Why?
- Can you be sure that you can't do it in fewer trips?
- What happens if you have more people (but still the same number of teachers as pupils)?

Torch and Bridge

Four people need to cross a river at night but there is only one torch. There is a bridge, but it can take only two people at a time. The torch is needed whenever crossing the bridge. The people walk at different speeds – this is how long each person takes:

Person	A	B	C	D
Time to walk across the bridge (minutes)	1	2	5	8

If two people cross the bridge together, they travel at the *slower person's* speed.
- What is the shortest time in which all of them can get across?
- Can you be sure that you can't do it more quickly?
- What happens if you change the times needed by the four people?
- What other *transport puzzles* like these can you invent?

46

Trapped Squares

Introduction

To become familiar with straight-line graphs it is helpful to sketch or draw accurately quite a few of them, but it is rather boring to make that an end in itself. In this lesson, there is plenty of opportunity for sketching graphs, while something more interesting is going on in the background; for learners already confident with drawing straight-line graphs, the investigation may move from the background to the foreground. For more details on the problem of the number of squares a diagonal passes through, including the extension to a *space* diagonal passing through cubes in *three* dimensions, see Branfield, J. R. (1969) 'An Investigation', *The Mathematical Gazette*, 53, (385), 240–7.

Aims and outcomes

- Draw or sketch straight-line graphs.
- Explore and justify patterns in a geometrical context.

Lesson starter (10 minutes)

Can you say the equation of a line that goes through (0, 5)? And another one, and another one?

Learners could give any equation with a y-intercept of 5, such as $y = 3x + 5$; in general, $y = mx + 5$, where m is a constant equal to the gradient of the line.

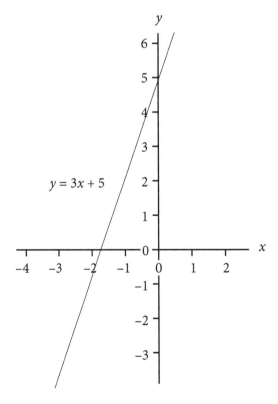

Can you say the equation of a line that goes through (5, 0)? And another one, and another one?

This may be harder, since now the x-intercept is given, which may be less familiar. One way to think of it is to switch x and y and give an equation such as $x = 3y + 5$; in general $x = ny + 5$, where n is a constant equal to the reciprocal of the gradient.

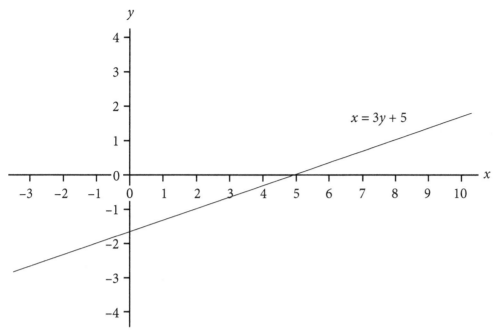

Can you say the equation of a line that goes through (0, 5) and (5, 0)? And another one, and another one?

This time there is only one possible answer, the equation $x + y = 5$, although learners might give this in different forms, such as $y = -x + 5$ or $2x + 2y = 10$.

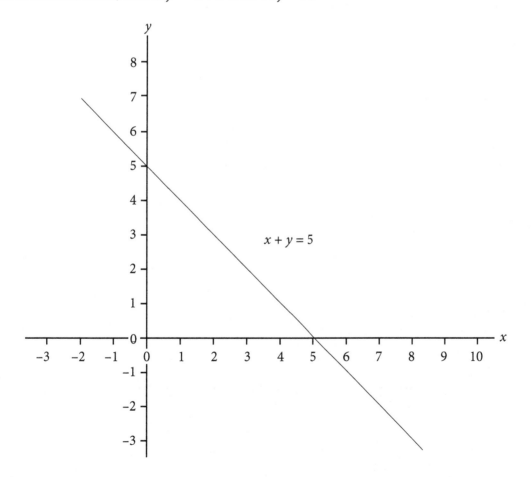

Main lesson (30 minutes)

Give out the Task Sheets and encourage learners to make accurate drawings of different straight-line graphs. Unless their graphs are accurate, they may obtain incorrect values for the number of squares underneath them. Graph-plotting software would be helpful, unless your main purpose is for learners to practise drawing these graphs for themselves.

Plenary (15 minutes)

What graphs did you try? How many trapped squares did you find? Did you find any connections between the equation of the graph and the number of trapped squares?

In general, for the line $y = mx + c$, if the gradient $m = 0$, we have horizontal lines, which do not enclose *any* squares (likewise with the family of *vertical* lines, $x = $ a constant). If $c = 0$, we have lines passing through the origin, which likewise do not enclose any squares. In all other cases, a region is defined, although of course it may not include any whole squares. If n is the number of trapped squares, then provided that m, c and $\frac{c}{m}$ are all positive integers, $n = \frac{c(c - m)}{2m}$. If m is *not* an integer, but is greater than 1, and $\frac{c}{m}$ is an integer (i.e. the line intersects both axes at integer coordinates) then the more complex formula $n = \frac{c(c - m - 1)}{2m} + \frac{1}{2}HCF\left(c, \frac{c}{m}\right)$ is needed.

This reduces to the first formula if $\frac{c}{m}$ is the highest common factor of c and $\frac{c}{m}$. In other situations, giving a formula for n is more difficult; one possibility is $\sum_{i=1}^{c-1}\left[\left\|\frac{c-i}{m}\right\|\right]$, where the vertical lines indicate 'modulus' (absolute value) and the square brackets indicate the 'floor function' (the greatest integer less than or equal to the quantity in the brackets). The situation where $m = 1$ and c is an integer gives the $(c - 1)$th triangle number, which can be seen visually or by substituting $m = 1$ into the formula $n = \frac{c(c - m)}{2m}$, giving $n = \frac{c(c - 1)}{2}$.

Homework (5 minutes)

Learners could continue their work or be invited to explore how the number of trapped squares varies in a *family* of equations, such as $x + 2y = k$, where k is a positive integer. The sequence for k beginning at 1 goes 0, 0, 1, 2, 4, 6, 9, 12, . . ., with differences +0, +1, +1, +2, +2, +3, +3, . . ., described by the formula $\left[\frac{(k-1)^2}{4}\right]$, where the brackets again indicate the 'floor' function.

To make it harder

Confident learners could try to find the largest area that encloses *no* whole squares. Alternatively, learners could try to find three graphs that enclose exactly four squares each, say, attempting to make their examples as 'different' as possible. Adventurous learners could also explore squares trapped by *curves*.

To make it easier

Beginning with diagonal graphs, in which $m = 1$, and varying c may be a helpful way to start if learners find this difficult. Learners could generate a table such as this:

Graph	Number of trapped squares
$y = x + 1$	0
$y = x + 2$	1
$y = x + 3$	3
$y = x + 4$	6

They may notice and be able to explain the triangle numbers obtained.

Trapped Squares

Here is the graph of $y = 2x + 5$.

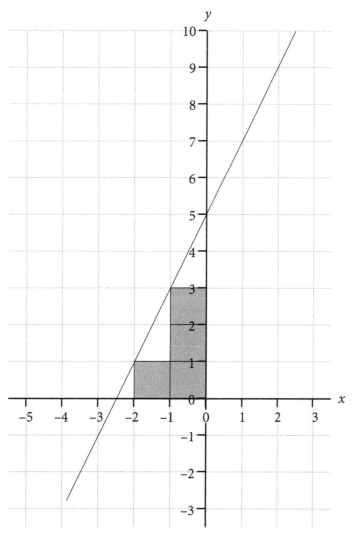

There are four whole unit squares '*trapped*' between the line and the axes.

Investigate the number of *trapped squares* for other graphs.

47 Travel Arrangements

Introduction

Learners often confuse displacement-time (or distance-time) graphs with velocity-time (or speed-time) ones. They also may interpret the diagram as a 'picture', showing a side-view of the motion, rather than as a graph plotting a certain variable against time. In this lesson, learners generate many possible shapes of graph by arranging four squares containing different lines and curves. Each can then be interpreted as either a displacement-time or a velocity-time graph and the motion described.

Aims and outcomes

- Draw and interpret travel graphs.
- Understand independent and dependent variables.
- Use graphs to model motion in one dimension.

Lesson starter (10 minutes)

Begin with a word-based task by writing the following on the board:

If my _____ is _____ then my _____ must be _____.

Point at the sentence and say:

If my displacement *is* constant *then my* velocity *must be* zero. *Why?*

Learners may need clarification of the meaning of words such as 'displacement'. They can then explain that a constant position means no movement, so zero velocity.

The first and third spaces can take these words: displacement, velocity, acceleration. (Write these on the board in one column.) *The second and fourth spaces can take these words: constant, zero, positive, negative, increasing, decreasing.* (Write these on the board in another column.)

How many different correct sentences can you make up? Why?

Learners could work on this in pairs, perhaps. There are five other possible correct statements.

1. Displacement, increasing, velocity, positive.
2. Displacement, decreasing, velocity, negative.
3. Velocity, constant, acceleration, zero.
4. Velocity, increasing, acceleration, positive.
5. Velocity, decreasing, acceleration, negative.

Learners may think, for example, that an increasing displacement implies a positive acceleration, but that is not true, since, for example, when a car is slowing down it continues to move forwards (increasing its displacement) until it stops. Sketching some graphs may help to make these ideas clearer.

Main lesson (30 minutes)

Give out the Task Sheets and some scissors. Learners should cut down the dashed line first and then cut along all the thin solid lines in the right-hand section. (Alternatively, these could be prepared beforehand and laminated.) Learners should first use the 'displacement' label for the vertical axis on the graph and then arrange the four square pieces to make a continuous graph. Then, in pairs, each learner should describe the motion of the object according to the graph. Then change the vertical axis label from 'displacement' to 'velocity' and swap so that the other person explains the *velocity*-time graph for the same arrangement. For example,

Displacement

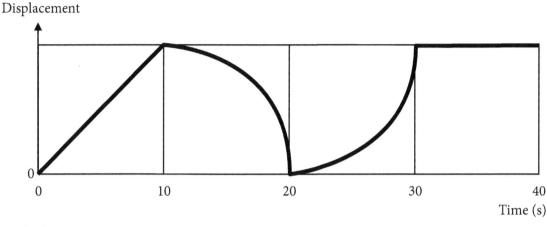

Velocity

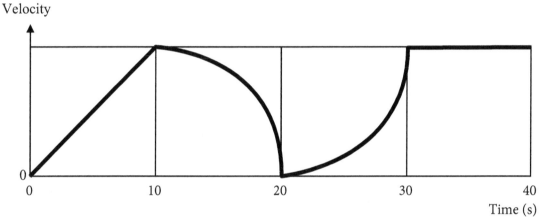

The object moves away at constant speed for 10 seconds, then suddenly stops and begins returning with increasing speed until it gets back to where it started after 20 seconds. It then begins to move away again with increasing speed until it reaches its maximum displacement again at 30 seconds. It stops here for the final 10 seconds.

The object accelerates away uniformly, reaching its maximum velocity after 10 seconds. Then it begins to slow down (not much to start with, but then very quickly), coming to a sharp standstill after 20 seconds. (It has travelled further in the last 10 seconds than it did in the first.) Then it begins to accelerate again, slowly at first, then fiercely, reaching its maximum velocity again after 30 seconds, which it maintains for the final 10 seconds. (It travels twice as far in the final 10 seconds as it did in the first 10 seconds.)

Plenary (15 minutes)

Which graphs did you make? Which did you find harder to interpret? Why?

All the pieces except the first can be placed in orientations in which at least part of the curve has infinite gradient, and this is likely to lead to useful discussion. Learners may also produce *discontinuous* graphs, which can also lead to useful discussion.

Did you find that any of your graphs described something impossible?

Realistic graphs need to be continuous, since the object cannot move instantaneously from one displacement to another without passing through all the intermediate positions. Graphs must be functions (i.e. they cannot be multi-valued) and they cannot have vertical asymptotes. Whether non-smooth changes are possible (i.e. vertices – kinks) is more debateable.

Homework (5 minutes)

Learners could be invited to make their own version of this task, with four squares containing lines or curves of their choice. Then they could combine these in, say, three different ways and write a sentence describing what is happening in each.

To make it harder

Confident learners could attempt to draw a velocity line (qualitatively – don't worry about the scale) superimposed on top of a given displacement-time graph. They could also try to extend this work to consider what *acceleration*-time graphs would look like.

To make it easier

Learners who find this hard could begin with the first and last (straight line) pieces, perhaps having two copies of each, before embarking on the pieces containing curves.

Travel Arrangements

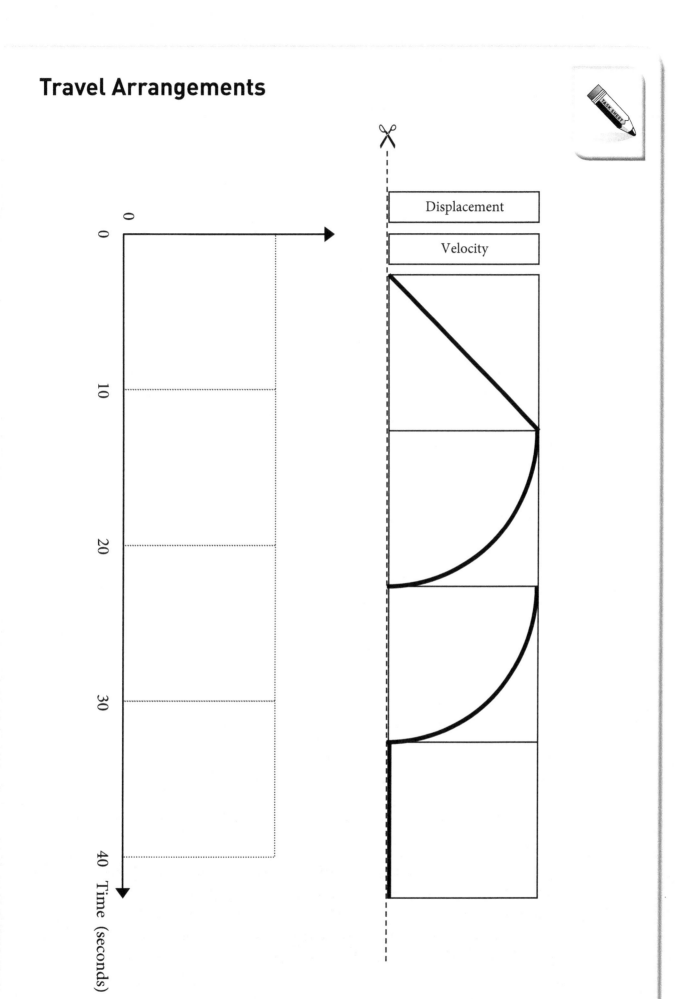

0

0

10

20

30

40 Time (seconds)

Displacement

Velocity

48

Triangle Angles

Introduction

The word 'trigonometry' literally means 'measuring triangles', and learners normally begin their study of this topic by finding the lengths and angles in lots of right-angled triangles. Since knowledge of the tan ratio is sufficient to find all of the angles in *any* triangle, given the coordinates of the vertices, in this lesson we use just the tan ratio to solve *non*-right-angled triangles. Learners need to look for right-angled triangles and then use them to find the angles in the *non*-right-angled triangles. This is an idea that can be extended to any polygon.

Aims and outcomes

- Solve *non*-right-angled triangles by breaking them into right-angled triangles.
- Use trigonometry to find angles and lengths in right-angled triangles.

Lesson starter (15 minutes)

Pick three lattice points (places with integer coordinates) that fit on this graph. (Three learners could choose a point each.)

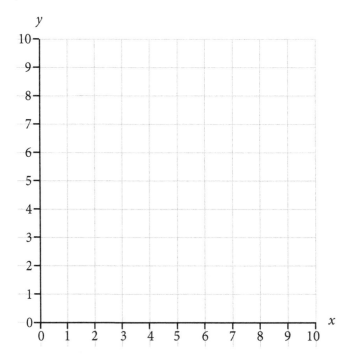

Join them up to make a triangle. (If the points happen to be collinear, that might be an interesting thing to talk about – then reject one of them and choose a fourth point that is not and use that.)

How could we find the sizes of the angles in this triangle?

Of course, we could measure with a protractor, but that is only approximate. Learners are unlikely to know about the cosine rule, which would be an alternative method of calculating the angles.

Suppose that the points are *A* (1, 3), *B* (4, 8) and *C* (6, 5):

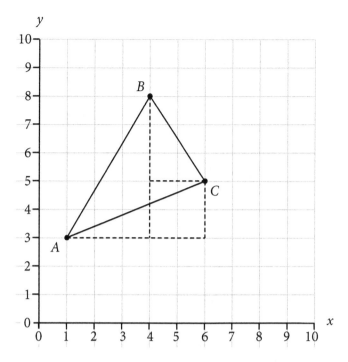

By making each side the hypotenuse of a right-angled triangle, as shown dashed above, we can calculate the angles:

$$A = \tan^{-1}\frac{5}{3} - \tan^{-1}\frac{2}{5} = 37.2°\text{ (correct to 1 decimal place)}$$

$$B = \tan^{-1}\frac{3}{5} + \tan^{-1}\frac{2}{3} = 64.7°\text{ (correct to 1 decimal place)}$$

$$C = \tan^{-1}\frac{3}{2} + \tan^{-1}\frac{2}{5} = 78.1°\text{ (correct to 1 decimal place)}$$

Learners may debate which of several possible similar triangles to draw; e.g. whether to use a 2 × 3 or a 4 × 6 triangle, and the fact that $\frac{3}{2} = \frac{6}{4}$, and therefore $\tan^{-1}\frac{3}{2} = \tan^{-1}\frac{6}{4}$, may help learners to see that it doesn't matter.

If you have a 'board protractor' handy (electronic or otherwise), you could verify these answers approximately. It is certainly worth checking that they add up (perhaps approximately, because of the rounding) to 180°. Since $\tan^{-1}\frac{a}{b} = 90 - \tan^{-1}\frac{b}{a}$, where $a, b \neq 0$, we know that they must add to up to 180° exactly, because:

$$A + B + C = (\tan^{-1}\frac{5}{3} + \tan^{-1}\frac{3}{5}) + (\tan^{-1}\frac{3}{2} + \tan^{-1}\frac{2}{3}) + (\tan^{-1}\frac{2}{5} - \tan^{-1}\frac{2}{5})$$

Main lesson (25 minutes)

Give out the Task Sheets and encourage learners to try different sorts of triangles (e.g. acute-angled, obtuse-angled, isosceles, etc.).

Plenary (15 minutes)

What triangles did you draw? What angles did you get? How did you calculate the angles? Were some trickier than others? Why/why not?

Triangles which are obviously right-angled leave only two angles to find. (Isosceles right-angled triangles must be 45°–45°–90°.) Isosceles triangles must have two equal angles, but unless their 'base' side is either horizontal or vertical, it may not be immediately obvious that the two angles are equal. With quadrilaterals, it is possible to have a reflex angle, which may need more care to find.

Homework (5 minutes)

Do you think you can draw an equilateral triangle with all its corners on grid points? Why/why not?

It is impossible in two dimensions, although it is possible in three dimensions, e.g. (0, 0, 0), (1, 1, 0) and (0, 1, 1):

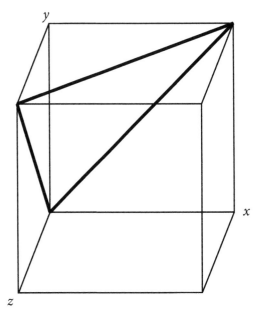

For an explanation of why it is impossible in two dimensions, see Beeson, M. J. (1992) 'Triangles with Vertices on Lattice Points', *The American Mathematical Monthly*, 99, (3), 243–52.

To make it harder

Learners who find this fairly straightforward could try the following.

Where do the lines y = 2x + 5 *and* y = 3x *meet? Why?*

What angles do they make where they meet? Why?

Try to generalise to other pairs of straight-line graphs.

The lines meet at (5, 15), as can be seen by inspection, by sketching the lines or by solving the equations simultaneously. But the angles they make when they meet depend only on the gradients, 2 and 3. Unless lines cross at right-angles, there will always be two different sizes of angle produced; in this case $\tan^{-1} 3 - \tan^{-1} 2 = 8.1°$ and $180 - (\tan^{-1} 3 - \tan^{-1} 2) = 171.9°$ (both correct to 1 decimal place). In general, the graphs $y = m_1 x + c_1$ and $y = m_2 x + c_2$ will intersect at right-angles if $m_1 m_2 = -1$; otherwise, they will intersect if $m_1 \neq m_2$ and make angles $|\tan^{-1} m_1 - \tan^{-1} m_2|$ and $180 - |\tan^{-1} m_1 - \tan^{-1} m_2|$. If $m_1 = m_2$ then the graphs are either parallel or exactly the same line, if $c_1 = c_2$.

To make it easier

Learners who have difficulty with this could begin with right-angled triangles in which one side is horizontal and one is vertical. They can then imagine moving one of the vertices to destroy the right angle and look at what happens.

Triangle Angles

Draw some triangles on the grid below. All the vertices must be on grid points.

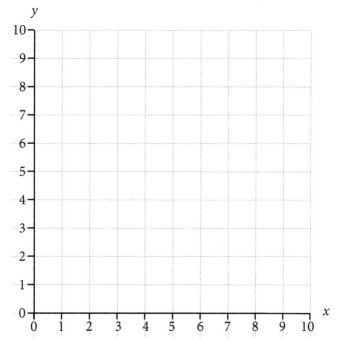

Use trigonometry to work out each of the angles inside your triangles.
Check that they add up to 180° each time.

Do you think it is easier to calculate the angles for some triangles than for others? Why/why not?

Now draw some *quadrilaterals* on the grid and calculate their angles.
Check that they add up to 360° each time.

What different kinds of quadrilaterals can you draw?
Do you think it is easier to calculate the angles for some of them than for others? Why/why not?

© Colin Foster (2011)   *Resources for Teaching Mathematics 11–14.* London: Continuum

49

Vanishing Lines

Introduction

Optical illusions can be a great way of creating cognitive conflict, something puzzling that learners need to resolve. In this lesson, a simple diagram, when cut out and rearranged, appears to produce an additional line segment. Learners' tacit beliefs in 'conservation of length' will be enough to create bewilderment, which they can then think about how to resolve. For more optical illusions, see Menkhoff, I. (2010) *Optical Illusions: Amazing Deceptive Images – Where Seeing Is Believing*. USA: Parragon.

Aims and outcomes

- Examine the area and the perimeter of shapes.
- Use gradient to solve a geometrical problem.

Lesson starter (10 minutes)

Do you see anything strange in this diagram? (It is drawn accurately.)

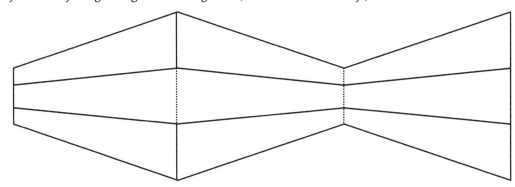

Make some conjectures about the lengths and angles.

Learners may comment on lines that they think are parallel or line segments or angles which look equal. The drawing is quite deceptive; in particular, the two dotted line segments are equal in length, but most people think the right-hand one looks longer. Learners might be able to explain how they think the illusion works, if they agree that the drawing is deceptive.

Main lesson (30 minutes)

Give out the Task Sheets and encourage learners to cut *only* along the thicker lines! Then they need to count the vertical line segments carefully. Can they see what is happening? Typically, learners are very surprised – disturbed, even – by this trick! Try to channel that energy into sorting out how it can happen.

Plenary (15 minutes)

Can you describe what happened? Did it surprise you? Can you make sense of it now?

Initially there are 13 vertical line segments, not counting the edges of the paper (the thick lines, which we cut along).

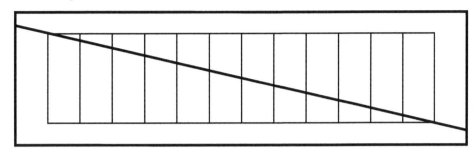

After sliding horizontally, there are *14* vertical line segments, again not counting the edges of the paper.

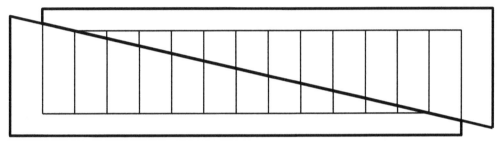

Observant learners may realize that the paper is not quite as tall after the slide, so the 12 innermost vertical line segments are slightly shorter than the original 13 ones before the slide. In fact, each one is $\frac{11}{12}$ as large, so the 12 of them together make a total of 11 original lines, leaving the ones at the end to make it up to the 13 we had at the start. We haven't lost any line length; it is just arranged differently.

If the original line height is h, then the gradient of the diagonal line is $\frac{h}{12}$, since there are 12 spacings (taken as unit length) between the 13 lines. This is still the same after the slide. There is conservation of total area and also conservation of total vertical line length.

Homework (5 minutes)

Find out about dissection puzzles/paradoxes and optical illusions on the internet. Be ready to show/ explain one next lesson.

For example, if you cut up the 8 × 8 square as shown on the left below, and rearrange the pieces, you obtain the 5 × 13 rectangle shown on the right. But 8 × 8 = 64 and 5 × 13 = 65.

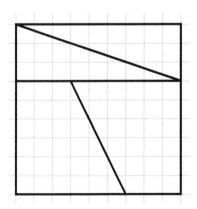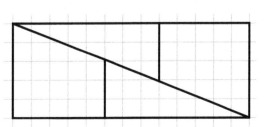

To make it harder

Confident learners could try to find the 'best' possible number of rectangles to use to make the illusion as convincing as possible. Too few, and the trick is obvious; too many and lining up the lines becomes too fiddly.

To make it easier

Making a version with fewer rectangles (fewer line segments) makes the illusion more obvious, so would be one option for learners totally stuck and unsure what to do.

Vanishing Lines

Cut around the *outside rectangle* of the diagram below.

How many vertical lines are there in the drawing?

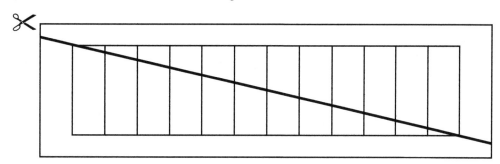

Now cut along the *thick diagonal line*. Don't cut along any other lines.

Slide the two pieces horizontally until the lines match up.

How many vertical lines are there now? Why?

Try making a shorter or longer version of this trick.

Do you think they work as well? Why/why not?

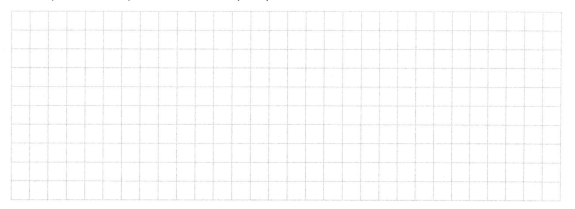

50

Water

Introduction

There are many prevalent misconceptions concerning volume, surface area and length, and this lesson may raise several as it involves learners in thinking about the effect on the depth of water in a tank when heavy objects of fixed volume are added. This has the makings of a practical problem: how much rubbish can we dump in rivers and the sea before the water level rises significantly – not to mention the many other obvious health and environmental concerns associated with doing this? There are many interesting (and alarming) water-related facts at: http://waterwise.sebenza-hosting.com/

Aims and outcomes

- Calculate volumes using given information.
- Estimate how lengths are affected by changes in volume.

Lesson starter (15 minutes)

Do you think that everyone in the school could get into the swimming pool at once?

    If they could, do you think it would overflow? Why/why not?

    What if they all crouched down under the water's surface? How much water would spill out?

If the pool is $50\,\mathrm{m}$ by $25\,\mathrm{m}$, then the area of the water's surface $= 50 \times 25 = 1250\,\mathrm{m}^2$. For a school with 1000 learners, that would allow $\frac{1250}{1000} = 1.25\,\mathrm{m}^2$ per person, or a square with sides of $\sqrt{1.25} = 1.1\,\mathrm{m}$, so a bit a tight to swim about but enough room to stand. (This could be a problem for those in the 'deep end', though!)

If everyone ducked under the surface of the water at once, then taking an average human volume as 70 litres, that would give an extra volume of $1000 \times 70 = 70\,000$ litres $= 70\,\mathrm{m}^3$, and over an area of $1250\,\mathrm{m}^2$, that results in a rise of the water of $\frac{70}{1250} = 0.056\,\mathrm{m}$, i.e. about $6\,\mathrm{cm}$ – probably less than learners might think! (Notice that the *depth* of the swimming pool makes no difference to this calculation, provided that there is enough room under the water for everyone to crouch down!)

    What if everyone on the earth *went swimming in the seas all at once? How much do you think the oceans would rise?*

This time some data will be needed. There are approaching 7 billion people in the world and the total surface area of the world's seas is around $3.5 \times 10^{14}\,\mathrm{m}^2$. This means that at 70 litres per person, if everyone got in that would represent an additional volume of $70 \times (7 \times 10^9)$ litres $= 4.9 \times 10^8\,\mathrm{m}^3$ which, when spread over all the seas, would correspond to an average rise of about $\frac{4.9 \times 10^8}{3.5 \times 10^{14}} = 1.4 \times 10^{-6}\,\mathrm{m}$, or about a thousandth of a millimetre! Notice that this small amount is not due to the vast depths of the oceans but to their enormous *surface area*.

Main lesson (20 minutes)

Give out the Task Sheets and encourage learners to read the information carefully. They need to understand that the cubes are not *floating* on the water – they are made of material sufficiently heavy to sink.

Plenary (20 minutes)

What answers did you get? Did anything surprise you?

Since the total area of the cross-section of water parallel to the front of the tank must be constant (because no water is lost), the height h_1 of the water after the first cube has been dropped in is given by $100 \times 1 = 98h_1$, so $h_1 = \dfrac{100}{98} = 1.02$ cm (correct to 3 significant figures). In general, after the nth cube has been added, $100 \times 1 = (100 - 2n)h_n$, so the height $h_n = \dfrac{100}{100 - 2n} = \dfrac{50}{50 - n}$, so the heights (correct to 3 significant figures) are:

n	h_n (cm)	n	h_n (cm)	n	h_n (cm)
1	1.02	11	1.28	21	1.72
2	1.04	12	1.32	22	1.79
3	1.06	13	1.35	21	1.72
4	1.09	14	1.39	22	1.79
5	1.11	15	1.43	23	1.85
6	1.14	16	1.47	24	1.92
7	1.16	17	1.52	25	2.00
8	1.19	18	1.56		
9	1.22	19	1.61		
10	1.25	20	1.67		

The height will reach 2 cm when $2 = \dfrac{50}{50 - n}$, so $50 - n = 25$, so $n = 25$. Beyond this many cubes, water will overflow the tank, so our formula is valid only for $n \le 25$. Notice that we need 25 cubes because that is sufficient to cover half the base of the tank, and halving the base area of the water doubles its height.

Learners could plot a graph of their results and comment on the shape.

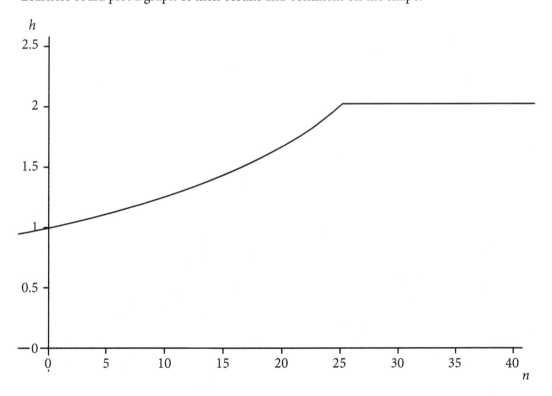

The graph is part of a hyperbola up to the point where $n = 25$, and then it becomes a horizontal line, since the water cannot rise beyond the 2 cm top of the tank.

Homework (5 minutes)

A well-known coffee shop chain was recently accused of wasting more than 23 million litres of water each day because the staff had been told to leave the taps running continuously to prevent the build-up of bacteria. Do you think that 23 million litres can be right? Do you think it is a lot of water? Why/why not?

The coffee shop chain has over 17 000 stores worldwide, so that is 1500 litres per store per day or about 100 litres per hour or 2 litres per minute, depending how long they are open. Since 2 litres is a large bottle, and you might be able to fill one in a minute with a steady flow of water, this estimate seems plausible. Supposing that a person uses 150 litres of water per day, each coffee store is using enough water for 10 people every day.

To make it harder

Confident learners could consider the problem in a 100 cm × 100 cm *square-based* tank, with the same height of 2 cm. This time adding a cube has a much smaller impact. The volume of water is constant, so $100^2 \times 1 = (100^2 - 2^2)h_1$, so $10\,000 = 9996h_1$, giving $h_1 = \dfrac{10\,000}{9996} = 1.000\,4$ cm (correct to 5 significant figures). In general, after the nth cube has been added, $10\,000 = (10\,000 - 4n)h_1$, so $h_n = \dfrac{10\,000}{10\,000 - 4n} = \dfrac{2500}{2500 - n}$. To raise the water level to the top of the tank, we need $2 = \dfrac{2500}{2500 - n}$, so $2500 - n = 1250$, so $n = 1250$. Notice again that this many cubes will cover exactly half of the base of the tank – and halving the base area will double the height.

Confident learners could also consider this classic puzzle: *An anchor is dropped from a small boat on a very small lake. Does the level of the lake rise, fall or stay the same? Why?*

While it's in the boat, since the boat-and-anchor is floating, it displaces a volume of water equal in weight to its weight (*Archimedes' principle*). Once it's dropped into the water, it sinks and displaces a volume of water equal to its *volume*, which is much less, since the anchor is much denser than the water (that's why it sinks). Since it's now displacing less water, the level of the lake falls (ever so slightly!).

To make it easier

Learners might benefit from handling a cardboard box and some cubes, although water would probably not be necessary, and could be problematic.

Water

Suppose you have a tray of water 100 cm long by 2 cm wide and 2 cm deep.
It is half-filled with water, so the depth of water is 1 cm.

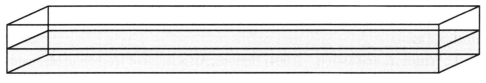

(Diagram not drawn to scale)

You have a large number of heavy 2 cm × 2 cm × 2 cm solid cubes.

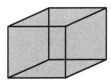

You place one cube into the water.

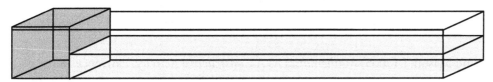

How much does the water level rise? Why?

What happens when you place a second cube next to the first? Why?

How does the water level change each time you add a cube? Why?
How many cubes will it take before the water reaches the top of the tray? Why?

What do you think happens with different sizes of tanks and cubes? Why?

Other Resources

Association of Teachers of Mathematics (1989) *Points of Departure 1–4*, Association of Teachers of Mathematics, Derby.

Bills, C., Bills, L., Watson, A. and Mason, J. (2004) *Thinkers*, Association of Teachers of Mathematics, Derby.

Mason, J. (1999) *Learning and Doing Mathematics*, QED, London.

Mason, J, and Johnston-Wilder, S. (2004) *Designing And Using Mathematical Tasks*, Open University, Milton Keynes.

Ollerton, M. (2009) *The Mathematics Teacher's Handbook*, Continuum, London.

Ollerton, M. (2005) *100 Ideas for Teaching Mathematics*, Continuum, London.

Ollerton, M. (2002) *Learning and Teaching Mathematics Without a Textbook*, Association of Teachers of Mathematics, Derby.

Ollerton, M. and Watson, A. (2001) *Inclusive Mathematics 11–18*, Continuum, London.

Watson, A. (2006) *Raising Achievement In Secondary Mathematics*, Open University, Milton Keynes.

Watson, A. and Mason, J. (2005) *Mathematics As A Constructive Activity*, Lawrence Erlbaum, New Jersey.

Other Books by Colin Foster

Foster, C. (2011) *Flowchart Investigations*, Mathematical Association, Leicester.

Foster, C. (2011) *Ideas For Sixth-Form Mathematics Lessons: Further Pure Mathematics and Mechanics*, Association of Teachers of Mathematics, Derby.

Foster, C. (2011) *Ideas For Sixth-Form Mathematics Lessons: Pure Mathematics and Statistics*, Association of Teachers of Mathematics, Derby.

Foster, C. (2010) *Resources For Teaching Mathematics: 14–16*, Continuum, London.

Foster, C. (2009) *Mathematics For Every Occasion*, Association of Teachers of Mathematics, Derby.

Foster, C. (2008) *50 Mathematics Lessons: Rich and Engaging Ideas for Secondary Mathematics*, Continuum, London.

Foster, C. (2008) *Variety In Mathematics Lessons*, Association of Teachers of Mathematics, Derby.

Foster, C. (2003) *Instant Maths Ideas for Key Stage 3 Teachers: Data, Numeracy and ICT*, Nelson Thornes, Cheltenham.

Foster, C. (2003) *Instant Maths Ideas for Key Stage 3 Teachers: Number and Algebra*, Nelson Thornes, Cheltenham.

Foster, C. (2003) *Instant Maths Ideas for Key Stage 3 Teachers: Shape and Space*, Nelson Thornes, Cheltenham.

Web Resources

An excellent website for stimulating learners' mathematical thinking is http://nrich.maths.org/.

There are many other excellent books and resources available from www.atm.org.uk.

Index

Numbers refer to *Lesson* numbers, not page numbers.

acceleration 47
aeroplane 3
affine transformations 44
air molecules 39
algebra 21, 34, 43
alphabet, letters of 38
always, sometimes and never 29
angle 26, 40
    exterior 7, 36
    in a triangle 48
    interior 36
    measuring 48
    polygons 7
    reflex 36
ape index 41
approximation, of pi 4
area 25, 26, 49
    of a circle 4
    of a triangle 4
arithmetic, modular 34
art 3
art gallery problem 40
assumptions 39
averages 6
Avogadro's number 39

balance 9
bar charts 20
bearings 16
binary numbers 9
birthday problems 12
bleep test 37
body language 15
body proportions 41
body-mass index 41
books 21
brackets, simplifying 34
breathing 39
broken calculator 9
butterfly 3

Caesar, Julius (100 BCE – 44 BCE) 39
cake numbers 2
cakes 2
calculator, broken 9
camels 31
CCTV cameras 40
circle 4
    area of 4
    equation of 3
    running in a 37

    sectors of 25
    unit 33
classifying polygons 29
codes 16, 20
Collatz Conjecture 14
combinations 9, 28, 47
commutativity 24
concave polygons 36
conditions, dual 27
consecutive numbers 43
constraints 45
convergence 14
converting units 12
coordinates 16, 19, 33
    integer 17, 48
    systems 16
cosine 33
Countdown 18
curves 3
cuts 22
cyclohexane 27

data
    collecting 41
    representing graphically 20
date 23
decimals, recurring 14
definitions, inclusive 29
denominators 42
desert, travelling across 11
Diophantine equations 8, 32
displacement 47
dissection 4
    paradoxes 49
distance 11, 13, 16, 37, 47
divisibility 34
division 28, 31, 34
Dragon curves 7
dual conditions 27

earth 13
Edison, Thomas (1847–1931) 39
Egyptian Fractions 2, 31
equations
    circle 3
    Diophantine 8, 32
    linear 8, 37
    quadratic 14
    simultaneous 17, 32, 37
    straight lines 19
equiangular polygons 27

equilateral polygons 27
equivalent fractions 42
estimation 13, 41, 50
Euler totient function 42
even numbers 43
expressions, simplifying 34, 43
exterior angles 7, 36

factor trees 5
factors 8, 35, 42
fairness 2, 25, 31
Fermat's Last Theorem 35
Fermi problems 39, 50
folding, paper 7, 22
Fortress problem 40
fractions
    addition and subtraction 2, 31
    equivalent 42
    reducible 42
    unit 31
frequency analysis 20
Friday 13th 12
functions, trigonometric 33

Gallivan, Britney (b. 1985) 7
Gauss Circle Problem 4
generalizing 43
geometrical patterns 19
gradient 49
graphs
    drawing 3, 44
    real-life 50
    sinusoidal 33
    straight-line 17, 19, 44, 46
    transforming 44
    travel 37, 47
grid 10, 16
Group theory 38
Gulliver's Travels 41

head 3
hex numbers 30
hexagons 30
hotels 10
hypotheses, statistical 41

iceberg 39
illusions, optical 49
imagination 4
inclusive definitions 29
infinity 14
integer coordinates 17
interior angles 36
iteration 23

journeys 16

kaleidoscope 15
Kawasaki's Theorem 7
kinaesthetic mathematics 33

ladder problems 17
Lagrange's Four-Square Theorem 35
lazy caterer's sequence 2
letters of the alphabet 38
line, vanishing 49
linear equations 8
lipograms 20
locus 11
logic 29, 45
Logo 36
loss function 7

Maekawa's Theorem 7
magic squares 10
manipulation of statistics 6
maps, folding 7
mass 9
matchstick problems 30
mathematical symbols 38
maximization problems 11, 45
mazes 1
mean 6
measurement 41
mega- 12
mental calculations 18, 24
messages 20
metric time 12
minimization problems 11, 40, 45
mirrors 15
modular arithmetic 34
mountain folds 7
multiples 8
museums 40

necessary and sufficient conditions 27
newspapers 21
normality 41
number(s)
    Avogadro's 39
    binary 9
    consecutive 43
    even 43
    hex 30
    large 39, 50
    obstinate 28
    odd 43
    palindromic 23
    prime 42
    small 39
    square 30, 35
    tetrahedral 30
    triangle 30

obstinate numbers 28
odd numbers 43
operations, priority of 18
optical illusions 49
origami 7
oscillations 33

pagination 21
palindromes 1, 23
paper folding 7
paradoxes, dissection 49
partitioning 2, 28
Pascal's Triangle 1
patterns, geometrical 19
people mathematics 33
percentages 24
perimeter 25, 26, 49
pi, approximation 4
Pick's Theorem 4
pictures 3
pizza 25
plans 26, 40
playground 40
Polignac conjecture 28
polygons 7, 22, 26, 40
    classifying 29
    concave 36
    regular 27
    star 36
possibilities 10
possibility tables 38
postcard trick 22
prime factorization 5
prime numbers 42
priority of operations 18
probability 34, 39
proofs without words 34
proportion 31
    body 41
puzzles, dissection 49
Pythagoras' Theorem 4

quadratic equations 14
quadrilaterals, classifying 29

ratio 31, 41
real life 2, 6, 11, 13, 17, 24, 25, 26, 28, 39, 50
rectilinear shapes 26
recurring decimals 14
reducible fractions 42
reflection 15
remainders 34
riddles 29
right-angled triangles 48
rooms 40
rounding 28
routes 1
running in a circle 37

scale factors 25
scales 9
school trip 45
sectors of circles 25
sequences 14, 21, 25, 35, 46
    from drawings 30
    integer 30
    surprising 28

shapes 29
    rectilinear 26
    within shapes 30
sharing 28
simplifying
    expressions 34, 43
    surds 35
simultaneous equations 17, 32, 37
sine 33
speed 11, 37, 47
spelling 1
square(s) 22, 34
    magic 10
    numbers 30, 35
    pandigital 35
    sums of 35
    trapped 46
'squircle' 22
standard form 39
star 22
    polygons 36
statistics
    hypotheses 13, 41
    manipulation of 6
straight-line graphs 17, 19, 44, 46
strategy 40
subsets 29
sums of squares 35
surds, simplifying 35
surprise 28
surveys 13
sweets 28
symbols, mathematical 38
symmetry 22, 36, 38

tables, possibility 38
tailor's rule of thumb 41
tangent 33, 48
teachers 40
tetrahedral numbers 30
time 11, 37, 47
    metric 12
Titanic iceberg 39
torch and bridge problem 45
totient function 42
transformations 15
    affine 44
    of graphs 44
transport problems 45
trapped squares 46
travel graphs 37, 47
triangle(s)
    angles in 48
    area of 4
    numbers 30
    right-angled 48
trick, postcard 22
trigonometric functions 33
trigonometry 48

unit fractions 31
units, converting 12

valley folds 7
vanishing line 49
variables 3, 47
velocity 47
Venn diagrams 27, 29
Vitruvian Man 41
volume 50

water
    molecules 39
    volume 50
    wasting 50
weight 9
Wiles, Andrew (b. 1953) 35
wolf, goat and cabbage problem 45
words 1, 16

Lightning Source UK Ltd.
Milton Keynes UK
UKOW05f0132101017

310714UK00005B/96/P

9 781441 142276